from the same Quiver

KATE VREDEVOOGD

A confessional tale of wanderlust, friendship and the pursuit of self-identity

From the Same Quiver

Copyright © 2019 by Kate Vredevoogd, Wanderlust Words Press

For permission requests, visit www.katevredevoogd.com

Ordering Information:

Quantity sales. Special discounts are available on quantity purchases by corporations, associations, and others. Orders by U.S. trade bookstores and wholesalers. For details, contact the publisher at the address above.

Editing by The Bookish Fox and Samantha Rodriguez
Cover Design by Miette Bennich
Interior Design by IAPS.rocks
Frente H1 font on the cover attributed to ShareAlike 3.0 Unported

ISBN: 978-1-7341839-0-0
1. Main category—TRAVEL/Special Interest/Literary
2. Other category—BODY, MIND & SPIRIT/Inspiration & Personal Growth
First Edition

Table of Contents

United States of America

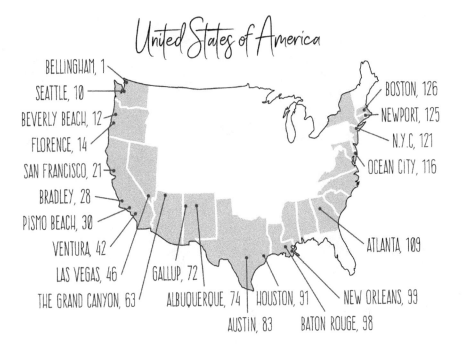

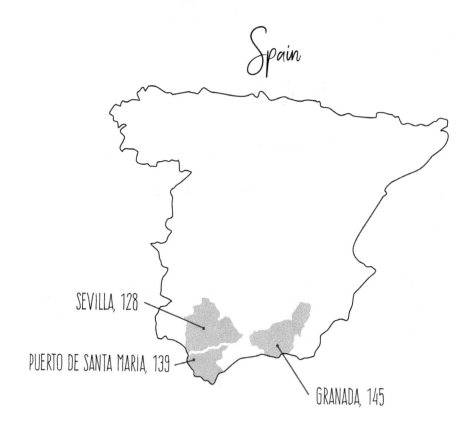

Spain

SEVILLA, 128

PUERTO DE SANTA MARIA, 139

GRANADA, 145

To Miette, and every other restless soul with
an unquenched thirst for adventure.
To every person who has tried to conform and failed.

What if it's the there
and not the here
that I long for?
The wander
and not the wait,
the magic
in the lost feet
stumbling down
the faraway street
and the way the moon
never hangs
quite the same.

—Tyler Knott Gregson, *Chasers of the Light:
Poems from the Typewriter Series*

Forward

By Miette Bennich

I CANNOT EXPLAIN WHAT MY BOND is with Kate when there is no word to describe it. "Friends" is too vague and shallow a description; "soulmates" seems romantic and dramatic; "sisters" is cluttered with both familial baggage and is cliché. The term "best friend" seems too obvious and quaint because even if that's what we had been before our grand adventure, we reached whatever comes after "best friend" by the end of it.

Kate and I met when we were in kindergarten, and even then she was highly intuitive and aware. She could easily guess the motivations of others, anticipate how certain events would transpire, and always held her cards close to her heart. She was also incredibly beautiful, which joined with her intelligence and drive for transformation, became a key that unlocked all sorts of doors. I possessed none of these qualities. Nevertheless, my quirkiness and infinite optimism blessed me with a unique charm that just barely hid a determination to achieve my staggeringly idealistic dreams. I have no doubt that many who witnessed Kate and I together wondered to themselves how such an odd pair came to be, and yet a pair we were.

There is one memory that stands out from our early teens as the perfect snapshot of who we were—two arrows from the same quiver.

Radio fuzz blasted from the one speaker in my dad's Ford Escort and lyrics to an alternative rock song could be heard through the static haze. We careened down the country road toward our favorite spot to hike, which began with a graveled parking lot in a field and ended at a wild and mystical forest at the end of the logging roads. Upon reaching the parking lot, we popped out of the car and started up the trail.

"Watch out for cougars," Kate cautioned, pointing to a sign on a fence post warning that cougars had been recently spotted in the area.

Once the trail met the logging road, the true hike began: both physically and mentally. Kate, as always, brought the cigarettes, which she was still too young to buy, as well as tales of late nights, much older boyfriends, and complicated social situations to untangle and interpret. For a long time, I wasn't sure what it was that I brought.

We left the logging road and ventured up a deer trail into the deep, dark forest. We were anything but lost little girls. We'd both grown up under the looming black conifers of the Pacific rainforest, and the wilderness was our comfort zone.

After an hour or so of walking, we turned around and headed back down to the car. I nearly missed the fresh rolled-up deer hide set to the side of the trail about fifty feet from the parking lot. With absolutely no consideration as to whose it was or why it was there, my vegan ass swept down to pick it up.

"Kate, I have to tan this," I shouted breathlessly. I had no idea how to tan anything.

Without so much as a perplexed blink, Kate grabbed one end and helped me haul it down the trail. I opened the hatch-back and pulled out an empty feed sack. As I carefully stuffed the hide inside of it, Kate peeked through the passenger window of the truck we were parked next to.

"We better go, hun. I think we just stole something from the dude who owns this truck, and I do not want to meet him."

Moments later, we were once again careening down the road, singing to the radio static. A stolen deer hide thumped around in the back, and an empty water bottle and pack of cigarettes rested on the dash.

The Beginning

EVERY DAY I WOULD GO through the same motions. I would open and close the bar, race down to last call in the local watering hole, sleep in too late, maybe squeeze in a trip to the gym depending on how late that after work drink went, and then rinse and repeat.

From the outside, I had it all. Being the bar manager, I made my own schedule and took pleasure in leading the team and having that coveted decision-making authority. On top of everything, I went home each night with a wad of cash in my pockets thanks to my faithful regulars. I lived alone in an apartment downtown, fully equipped with a flat screen TV, beautiful furniture that I had collected secondhand, and a walk-in closet brimming with clothes and shoes. At any given moment, I could walk out my door to the downtown sidewalk and find a group of familiar faces to grab a drink and hang out with, but every day I asked myself, *Why is this not enough? What is this void inside of me?* It was as if a black hole in the depths of my chest were sucking up my life energy and leaving me a shell of a woman.

The truth was, I couldn't see beyond that rinse and repeat cycle. Everything was too easy and, recently, I had been feeling like I had lost my path and knew that something needed to change because boredom of routine and a lack of challenge were my two fiercest predators. I had dedicated the previous six years of my life to working in bars and casinos—which I was dangerously good at—and splashing around in the dark yet enticing waters of life after midnight. Living on the edge had always been something at which I excelled, but I had been dancing along the line of healthy experimentation and perilous recklessness for long enough to know that I would eventually lose my balance and fall crashing down.

One day, deep in the throes of my existential crisis, I was sitting in the big leather armchair in the living room of my parents' house in the countryside, thinking about why I didn't feel fulfilled.

"I just feel like I don't have art. Or, I mean, I *do* have art, but what I don't have is a way to express it," I said, gazing out the large windows at the evergreen forest and the fields that surrounded our house.

My father was a musical man, always ears deep in some project, albeit playing bass guitar in an Afro-Cuban jazz band, making his own steel drums, or refinishing grand pianos. "I tried music, you know, and music is super important to me, but I just don't feel totally free when I'm playing the piano. It feels like work, you know? And sometimes like suffering," I said, laughing a little. "I see all these naturally gifted musicians who go into this sort of rapture when they're playing, and I've never felt that."

"Well, don't you think they had to suffer to get to that point?" my mom said.

"Yeah, but it's just not my thing. I like it. I'll keep doing it, but it's not what I'm talking about. I want to feel liberated. I want to feel the art just, like, flowing out of me like it's what I'm on this earth to do, you know?"

There was a thick silence before my dad spoke.

"You're a writer."

He said these words with more conviction than I had ever said anything in my life. My mom nodded her support.

"I dunno, Dad. I think I'm a photographer."

I always have to be contrary, even when my company is on my side. Being the quintessential Libra that I am, I have a terrible time making decisions, and the more mundane the decision, the more I labor over it, weighing the pros and cons of each option. I am capable of spending half an hour in the shampoo aisle just trying to decide between two drugstore brands. Do I want more volume, or do I want to repair my split ends? What a consequential question!

When I found myself struggling excessively with any decision, I would often turn to my mother to help me. If it were between the blue dress or the black dress, when she said blue, I wore black. So when my parents told me that I was a writer, I automatically scratched that idea off of my list. It turned out that we were all right. Photography and writing are now the glue that holds the pieces of me together.

A few days after that conversation with my parents, I called Miette, my best friend, to meet me for lunch. Miette and I had become instant friends on our first day of elementary school, at the spritely age of five. We had spent our childhood barefoot with our hair in knots and our shins scratched and bruised from our afternoons whipping through the evergreen forests that surrounded our houses in the countryside, running from mythical beasts of our own creation. We found refuge together in fantasy, even into our adult years, and now at twenty-three we were still drawn to anything mystical. Miette was petite in stature and often reserved. She was the queen of nervous laughter, and she was capable of changing your life with one poignant observation, delivered with her trademark humor and awkwardness. Miette's occasional lack of social savvy and overly-apologetic nature could potentially be attributed to her post-kindergarten homeschooling.

She had been living in her apartment alone while her husband, on the other side of the country, was acclimating himself to his new job climbing cell towers in New Jersey.

"So I'm heading to Jersey soon," she said while we sipped sake in a remote corner of a Japanese restaurant near her house.

"Yeah? Are you excited?" I asked.

"I don't know if excited is the word. I think it's more like nervous. I mean, this is going to be like the final test."

"Yeah," I said, contemplating her words. "You guys have been having a tough time lately. Sucks watching you suffer."

"We'll see how it goes. Hopefully with a change of scenery, things will get better. I'm just so tired of everything being so hard." She wiped her eyes quickly with the back of her hand.

"Yeah, I get it. God knows I'm no relationship guru, but if you both want it to work out…" I trailed off. It was one of the rare occasions that I didn't have the right words to say.

She sighed.

"So how are you going to get there? And what are you going to do in Jersey?" I asked, struggling with my chopsticks. "I mean, he's living in a men's youth hostel, right? What's your plan?"

"That's the thing: I don't have one. But I'm ready for a change. I think I need it. Like, really, what am I even doing with my life right now?"

As she spoke, I couldn't help but ask myself the same question. What was I doing with my life? We spent the next half hour discussing how life was feeling more and more like quicksand, sucking us deeper into service-industry jobs and wasted university degrees. There had to be more out there for us, and maybe it was time to go and find it.

I had a college education but had so far only used it for bragging rights; my bar tips kept me too comfortable to consider any other career moves. I had finished university with a double major in linguistics and Spanish two years before when I was just twenty-one years old.

Just like with everything else in my life, I was a couple steps ahead of the crowd. I was the first of my friends to get a boyfriend. I was the first of my group to be expelled from junior high. I was also the first to get a part-time job, move out of my house, get a fake ID, and begin living life like the adult I thought I was. I had travelled around distant countries alone before many of my peers had even left the West Coast. I was the youngest student to begin Running Start, a program which allows kids to take community college courses for high school credits, and I was consequently the first among my peers to graduate from university with not one, but two degrees. I may also have been the first to get a DUI., to go to eight a.m. university classes drunk, and the first to be invited to stay after-hours to do lines of coke off of the dirty downtown bar tops.

In retrospect, I think it was about pushing limits, any and all limits, and an intrinsic need to shock not just other people but myself as well. But it had been a while since I had shocked anyone with a real achievement that I was proud of or pushed limits toward something positive. This was undoubtedly weighing on my self-esteem. I'm not sure where my need to take things to the extreme came from, but I do know that I would almost never say "no" to people, to adventures, to drugs, or to opportunities, and I rarely let people say "no" to me. "No" simply wasn't a word I had welcomed into my vocabulary.

"Miette, Miette, Miette, I just had an idea. Oh my god, I just had *the idea*. What if we drove to New Jersey? What if we just said, 'Fuck it' and took a road trip across the country?" I couldn't contain myself. I had struck gold, and the words couldn't come out of my mouth fast enough. The piece of tuna maki that was resting in the air between Miette's chopsticks fell to her plate with a thud, and her eyes, open wide and unblinking, rose to meet mine.

"Oh. My. God. That is the plan." We sat in silence for a few moments. "It was always the plan. We just didn't know it until right now," she said.

"Oh, and what if I did some kind of documentary photography piece about it? Like an exposé on American subculture?" I said, the good ideas just rolling in. "I know the street photography around America thing isn't super original, but I could play with the road trip element and find an angle. Don't you think that'd be cool?"

"Oh my God, Kate. You are on fire!"

We had a plan. But like the arrows we would tattoo on ourselves two weeks later, our plans were both different and the same. We were both suffering from identity crises and overwhelming feelings of blasé, but Miette would drive across the country looking to find stability in her marriage and a new home whereas I was looking to turn everything upside down and to get lost in something different, scary, challenging. Stability was my nightmare.

Miette and Sol had met in high school, and Sol had loved her from the moment he saw her, I was sure. Miette is a Sagittarius who would have flitted from one man to another for years before settling down if Sol hadn't courted her with such patience and integrity, winning her over completely and becoming her ultimate teammate in life and her perfect complement. They had been high-school sweethearts, and their young love blossomed throughout their teenage years, but something had happened in the last few years that had changed them.

They had been living in a yurt, basically off the grid in the forest, while Miette went to university. She chose a challenging major, biochemistry, and the pressures of school and finances aggravated her anxiety and obsessive tendencies. Their tough living conditions and having to coordinate her classes with a very limited bus schedule took their toll on her.

I saw her much less during those intense years, and every time we'd make plans, I was overcome by the excitement of finally spending time with my best friend. But when we were together, I noticed something different, like she was only partly there. It was like a tiredness had dampened her fire, and instead of the bright flame of a girl that I was used to, she had been reduced to a few sparsely glowing coals. That must have been when things started to change between her and Sol. How had I been so entirely out of touch with my best friend? How had I not realized that her candle had been burning at both ends, that she was working herself into a depression, and that the expectations that she was holding herself to were so demanding that they could only ever result in heart-wrenching feelings of failure and despair? She had been seeing the university therapist to try to manage her stress, but it was never clear to me how much of her stress was caused by her relationship nor to what degree her relationship was being affected by her stress.

I was also wrapped up with living my own stories at the time. I was taking classes all morning, studying in the afternoons, and working in the casino at night. On top of all that, I was also taking care of my then-boyfriend's two young children the three days of the week that we had them, not to mention dealing with more than my fair share of my signature boy drama. Miette and I had both taken the plunge into our twenties making a big splash, as we jumped quickly into as many complicated adult situations as we could. It was irrefutably more of a cannonball than a swan dive for both of us.

Growing up, she had always armed herself with such a strong exterior and was seemingly unafflicted by the toils and troubles of young relationships. Having found her soulmate at sixteen, what troubles was she going to have? She was the one who would always pick me up when I fell into endless depressions triggered by unhealthy relationships. She was my unwavering support when I moved out of my parents' house at seventeen and in with my twenty-three-year-old, alcoholic, guitar-playing, master-of-escapism boyfriend, and she was my cheerleader when I finally got out, only to then fall in love with a single father of two adorable rugrats, whose ex-wife was in and out of jail and couldn't stand the idea of my existence.

Miette and I would meet for walks up into the woods, Miette with her deck of tarot cards and me with candles and blankets. We would climb up into a little wooden structure in the trees behind the university campus between classes and set up our afternoon witching-hour ritual, looking for guidance in the drawings on the cards. Miette was my rock through all of the heartbreak, and now it was my turn to be hers.

Washington

A
S I ROLLED DOWN THE window to light a cigarette, the balmy, summer air rushed into the car, throwing my hair in every direction. A sense of overwhelming freedom held me in reverie. It was July 2013, just two weeks after our meeting for sushi, and Miette and I had been on the road for a whole ten minutes. My eyes followed the last exit for Bellingham sign as we sped south down the freeway, my heart pounding so hard it rattled the butterflies in my stomach. Everything important to me was in my backpack in the back seat of Miette's '96 Toyota Tercel. That was it. All of my ties were cut. All of my ex-boyfriends, drunken-late night embarrassments, quarrels with my family, whiskey-regrets and cocaine-friendships were behind me. I was driving away, just like in the movies.

We were nearing Seattle after almost two hours on the road. We arrived at Georgetown—a grungy, alternative district in South Seattle. We were a few minutes early for the appointment I had made for us at my favorite tattoo studio so we pulled up to the bar next door, the Georgetown Liquor Company. After two shots of tequila with a spicy tomato back, our commemorative tattoos went on like a breeze, and we were ready to leave Washington behind us.

"Do you realize that now you've been with me for my first piercing and my first tattoo?" Miette asked as we left the shop. "It's like...you help me be the person that I am, but I'm too afraid to be by myself."

I laughed but also wondered if I were the bad influence

friend, and not for the first time either. The black lines of the arrow she had put on her inner left bicep were raised and inflamed. I had put a similar, but not identical, one just under my left collarbone.

It is said that an arrow can only be shot by pulling it backward so when life is dragging you back with difficulties, it means that it's going to launch you into something great, so you should just focus and keep aiming. This was our mantra, and we now carried it with us, etched in our skin.

We drove south with our empty plastic Starbucks cups resting on the dashboard. The hot air stuck to my skin, and savage excitement filled the car. We had changed into our bikini tops in a gas station bathroom. I had my legs thrown up against the car door, and we made accidental eye contact with the wide-eyed men in the pickup trucks next to us after we noticed that they were matching our speed to get a better look at us. What was going to happen? What would we find during the next month? Would we find ourselves? Each other? I watched the evergreen trees fly past as we plunged into the unknown, trying to decide if what I felt was nervous excitement or sheer terror.

Oregon

WE STOPPED FOR DINNER IN Portland in what seemed like a cool bistro, but which ended up being expensive and pretentious. After our uneventful and uninspired meal we didn't delay getting back to our seven-hour journey.

"I wish Oregon would pick a damn speed limit," I huffed to Miette after we had exchanged the freeway for country highways and the signs changed yet again from fifty miles per hour to thirty.

"I know! It's like they want you to fail!"
I pulled out my phone to check the map. When I saw that we still had sixty miles to drive before we would reach our campsite and it was already evening, I lost a noticeable amount of my enthusiasm. The plan we had mapped out was really more of a guideline. Even more accurately, it had been an idea that had turned into a plan that was based on zero research and perhaps not enough common sense.

"Kate, look! It's the ocean. We made it back to the coast!" said Miette as if it had been months since we'd seen the water instead of just that morning. The sun set on our right as we drove through the evening and into the ebony night. Surrounded by the bulk of her car, which was solid and familiar, unlike the night outside, I felt like nothing could touch me. Reveling in the safety, I snuggled up in a little blanket I'd acquired years earlier in Mexico and leaned my head against the door to contemplate the stars. I pulled up the hood of my sweatshirt—not because I was cold, but to soften the vibration of the car door against my skull. When we saw the sign for Beverly Beach Campsite, the only light was the moon reflecting on the water behind us. We found our lot resting amidst the trees and total silence.

Delirious and disoriented from the hours we'd spent in the car, we shuffled around the darkness, trying to make a place to sleep. I grabbed the tent that Miette had brought, and, preparing myself for the always tedious task of setting it up, I unzipped the case. To my surprise, it erupted violently out of my hands, popping into a perfectly formed tent. I screamed for my life as I fell backward to the ground.

Miette choked out some words between gasps of laughter. "It's a pop-up tent." Tears were streaming down her face, and after she caught her breath, she added, "It probably smells weird since it hasn't been used since the eighties."

I grabbed two organic, gluten-free, raspberry beers from the ice chest. "Dude, how cliché Bellingham are we?" I said, referring to our choice of beers. They clearly came from a health food store, which were ubiquitous in our town. As I looked for a way to open the beers, I realized that we were the worst campers ever because we didn't even have a pocket knife. We couldn't be cliché Bellingham because people from Bellingham are expert campers; it's in their blood. We spent the rest of the night drinking in the shelter of our tent, telling ghost stories, laughing ourselves to hysterics, and clutching our pillows close.

I greeted the next morning dehydrated and sticky. I found myself tangled up in a pile of clothes and blankets and next to me was an empty bottle of sauvignon blanc. I was a disheveled mess with a pounding headache. If only that wine bottle hadn't been a twist off, we would have saved ourselves from a hangover.

For a brief moment I was expecting to start another normal day in Bellingham, but I was jolted back to reality by the nylon feel of the sleeping bag. I looked up at Miette to see her pixie haircut pressed down and sticking out. I also noticed that she had been cuddling three empty raspberry beer bottles and using a pair of jeans as a pillow.

"Coffee," she grumbled.

"Coffee now," I replied, and we burst into a delirious laughter as we started picking up the pieces of our lives that we had left haphazardly around the camp. A good Northwesterner would have a small gas stove and coffee already brewing.

The reality of the day was sharper and colder than the previous day. Things weren't as romantic. I gazed out the window at an overcast sky as we drove down the coast of Oregon. I looked over the cliffs at the crashing tides and felt connected to the great Pacific Ocean that had been such a presence during my twenty-three years on this earth. Was I leaving that ocean behind? When would I see it again after all of this was over? I was in a strange place—not physically but spiritually.

As we drove down the coast of Oregon, the grey sky opened up to reveal an electric blue. We found coffee, charged our phones, and ate a sandwich, and we had only been in the car for about an hour and a half when the beaches changed from rocky cliffs to sandy dunes. We pulled off onto a dirt road that went toward the water, and we parked the car in front of a big, golden hill. I kicked off my flip-flops and stepped out of the car before sinking my bare feet into the sand. I glanced at Miette and then up at the dune before taking off running.

I ran desperately and ungracefully, occasionally falling and sliding backward while grabbing a fistfull of sand as I tried to pull myself back up, until, out of breath, I reached the summit of the dune, from which I saw the vast Pacific spread out before me. I looked at Miette next to me, clutching her ribs while she caught her breath.

"Well that was a lot harder than it looked," she said.

"I know right? They could make a workout out of running up and down dunes."

Seagulls flew overhead, and the wind charged my body with energy and ecstasy; I felt alive. Nothing else apart from that moment in time had any importance, and there was no other place in the world where I would have rather been.

Equally as ungracefully as we had climbed the hill, we tumbled down the other side, smearing footprints in the sand behind us and racing to plunge our feet in the dark green water. We danced up and down the shore, letting our skin toast in the sun, without giving a second thought to the passing time.

"Miette, do we have to leave?" I whined. "I want to stay here forever."

She looked at me sadly and we both admitted that it was time to get back on the road.

We climbed into the car, both of us with a recovered *joie de vivre*, and continued south with the ambitious destination of San Francisco, which was over nine hours of driving away. Nearly two hundred miles, three pee stops, and many snacks later, we noticed the trees around us getting thinner and taller until we found ourselves surrounded by the quiet, noble redwoods of the Redwood National Park. The ocean on our right sat calmly below a dizzying cliff, and all around us the trees reached for the sky with a cloudy mist resting softly on their branches. We stopped the car to wander through the woods, and I was reminded of a verse from "Stopping by Woods on a Snowy Evening" by Robert Frost. It felt like a dream; there were most definitely fairies hiding nearby.

California

E CROSSED THE BORDER INTO California and followed the Redwood Highway in an awe-inspired stupor, basking in the magic all around us. We eventually pulled off at the beach to admire the sunset. The sun was a glowing pink orb just touching the perfect line of water on the horizon, and soon the blue hour was upon us. Despite the beautiful landscape we had before us, the impossible stillness of it all sent a chill feeling down my spine. I noticed a sign that said, "OREQ-W: An Ancient Yurok Village Site." Goosebumps crept up my arms as I looked at a few dilapidated wooden buildings. The place felt like it had stories to tell—important stories that I potentially wasn't ready to hear.

"Yeah, like anyone is going to have a picnic here," responded Miette sarcastically to a "Picnic Area" sign. "Way too many ghosts."

We followed Highway 101 down the coast and then through green fields. The fog was settling, and the light was getting dimmer when we passed a pasture of cows. The cows were motionless. There was a strange energy in the air.

The hours passed, and our desperation to finish the driving for the day began to grow. Suddenly, I was acutely aware of the silence in the car and how we would take turns yawning every few minutes. It was around midnight, but I had an idea. I pulled out my phone to look for a Walmart where we could buy the aux cable we needed to connect my iPhone to her car stereo. Music would definitely help revive us. We had been driving thus far with nothing but the sound of wind and our own voices, and we were both running out of things to say as well as the energy to say them. The sky was pitch black, and the Walmart parking lot was empty and unlit, except for one flickering, orange light whose post we parked right underneath. I could see the shadows of hundreds of moths flitting drunkenly around it.

After such a mystical evening, the bright, fluorescent lights and apathetic faces of the late-night Walmart shoppers reminded me of that moment when a dream segues into a terrible nightmare or a bad mushroom trip. We wandered up and down the aisles like mice in a maze. We saw pale-skinned, night-shift workers doing their weekly shopping, teenagers messing around because they weren't old enough to go to bars and needed somewhere to hang out, a scraggly-haired couple buying energy drinks and Marb light 100s. I felt entirely out of place. On our way out to the car, the young cashier who had checked us out followed behind us, shouting something unintelligible.

As he got closer, we heard, "Hey! Hey! What're ya girls doin'? I'm Brian and—"

"We have big plans, Brian," I said, cutting him off.

"Ah, yeah, 'cause I was just gonna say that if you were lookin' to get some weed or somethin', I can hook ya up. I got it all right here," he said, nodding toward his car, "and my apartment is just down the street if you wanna kick it."

"Yeah, that's cool. Thanks anyways though," I said as Miette scrambled for her keys and unlocked the car.

"Alright, well, you ladies have a good night. Peace!" He made the hang loose sign by making a fist with both of his hands and leaving his thumbs and pinkies extended. As he said his parting words, we shut the car doors.

I plopped down in the car. I had been making my little nest: lip balm in the door handle, purse between my feet, cell phone under the stereo, and a camera bag just behind me on top of the Tetris puzzle of Miette's various boxes and precious items.

Miette started the engine. Her Toyota Tercel was a manual, and I had never learned how to drive a stick-shift. Although she didn't seem bothered by having to drive the whole way, I was certainly bothered by not being able to help with the burden.

"Miette, teach me to drive stick," I said, as if it were something I could just pick up in a five minute lesson.

"Sure, okay," she answered, always up for an adventure. We traded places and I got into the driver's seat. As I positioned myself in the car, I felt awkward and didn't know where to place my feet. There were too many things to think about, and suddenly the mundane task of driving was a great, seemingly impossible challenge. After her initial explanation, I gave it a go and managed to lurch the car forward. On my next attempt, I got the Tercel rolling—and then shrieked when I realized I didn't know how to brake.

"I don't understand how this works, Miette," I whined, shaking the steering wheel in frustration, "and until I understand it, I'm not going to be able to do it, man!"

Miette understood it. She was a car person. She was one of those gals who could fix things when they broke, whereas I would just get frustrated and break them more. She was one of those self-sufficient women whom feminists smile at proudly. I, on the other hand, would either let things stay broken or just call a guy. My frustration quickly turned into amusement, and my yelling turned into defeated laughter. Miette, also giggling, admitted that maybe nighttime in the Walmart parking lot was not the best place to learn. I sighed, recognizing that it would be up to her to get us safely to New Jersey, and I accepted that this would be my first and last driving lesson in the Tercel.

It was time to discuss our short-term plan because San Francisco was still nearly four hours away and it was already past midnight. Would we drive through the night and wake up the next day in a bed in San Francisco or give in to the exhaustion and find a place to unpop the popup tent? We decided to power through. We blasted nineties rock, and I tried to be as entertaining as possible, but I could see that Miette's eyelids were heavy, and in that moment, I remembered something that could help.

"Miette," I spoke slowly, testing the waters, "I have some cocaine. A friend gave me some for the road as a sort of parting gift, and, well, we're on the road." I pulled a little baggy out of a tin where I had that and other treats stashed, and I grabbed my keys. I plunged one of the keys into the bag and scooped out some white powder. I looked over at her and waited for her blessing.

"Oh! Um, well, great," she said awkwardly, not sure exactly how to react. I didn't know the extent of her experience with the stuff. I knew she had never tried it but had definitely witnessed other people do it. I put the key close to my face and took in a sharp breath of air through my nose. I scooped out some more, this time much less, and again looked over at her.

"Did you want to try it?"

"I mean, it would help me stay awake, and it's still a long way to San Francisco." Her fearless reply took me by surprise. "How does it work?"

"Okay, so you're going to plug one nostril," I said, pressing my index finger to the left side of my nose, "and then suck in really hard through the other one. Then you wait for the burn to creep down your throat."

"But what will it do to me?"

"Think of the last time you had too much coffee. I mean, like, three cups too many of really strong coffee. Basically, you'll have a ton of really important things to say, and you'll say them really fast, like it was a race to get it all out, and after half an hour of that, you'll realize that you've just single-handedly solved all of the world's problems. And then, little by little, you'll start to feel sad and then embarrassed about everything you've just said. And then you'll either need to do more or wait for the crash to pass. It's actually quite awful, I don't know why people love it so much..."

"Alright. Let's do this thing," she said, not completely deterred by my speech, but with her left eyebrow slightly raised.

We stopped the car on the shoulder and I was poised, holding the key steadily near her face. "Ready? Okay. There are no cars. You're safe. Go for it."

She sniffed as hard as she could. "Oh my God. It burns! It's so gross!" Her nose crinkled up, and her eyes watered. After a few moments of choking and pained laughter, she pulled herself together, and we got back on the road.

"Man, I'm excited to see San Francisco. I can't believe we're going to San Francisco, Kate! This is so cool!" she said, pulling on the steering wheel in her enthusiasm.

"Yeah, I'm stoked too!"

"I've always wanted to go there. I mean, you see a place all the time in the movies, and then you go there, and it's like, woah, this is that place!"

I smiled and pulled out my phone to put on some house music.

"I don't think I'm feeling the coke. Or maybe I am. How will I know?" she asked.

"You never really know," I said, laughing. "That's why people always think they want more." Her innocence was always so endearing. "It's not like acid where suddenly the walls are swirling and plants grow faces or anything."

"Tercel is such a great little car. She's doing such a good job!" she gushed.

"Oh, for sure. She is a champion."

"And it is such a beautiful night! I mean, it's the perfect temperature." She stuck her hand out the window to feel the air. "God, I just can't believe this is all happening. We are doing it, Kate. We're actually doing it!"

"We're champions!" I shouted.

"This is the best idea we've ever had!"

"Best idea ever!"

"I think I might be feeling something now..." she said, pointing out the obvious. We continued for another half an hour, talking about how marvelous everything was, and then, when the high wore off, we drove awhile in somber silence. That's cocaine in a nutshell.

Hours passed, and the electro house music playing from my iPhone lulled us into a trance. I found myself again gazing into the stars, getting lost in the great expanse of sparkling dots in the sky and wondering how many other people were doing the same. Just as the stars are infinite, the stories of the people gazing up at them in that very moment must have been, too.

We were both deep in our worlds of introspection when suddenly two big poles and ropes emerged from the fog. We were about to cross the Golden Gate Bridge. I sat up, alert in my seat, and Miette adjusted her glasses and pulled herself close to the steering wheel. It was happening. We were finally, at 4:30 a.m., arriving at San Francisco. I had to snap out of my haze in order to navigate the foreign, one-way city streets. We drove around the same block over and over, first looking for the hostel and then looking for parking. It wasn't an easy battle after such a long day, but after about twenty minutes of wrong turns and traffic lights, we parked the car, grabbed our daypacks, and stumbled into the hostel, tripping over ourselves and bumping into everything in our path. We both sprawled out on our teeny bunk bed mattresses and didn't stir until the next morning.

I opened my eyes to see sunlight streaming in through the curtain and Miette's poof of hair peeking out from her blanket in the bed across from me. We were in the room alone with two bunk beds to ourselves. It must have been around eleven in the morning.

"Did you sleep good, pretty?" I asked her when I saw her poof moving around.

"Yeah...last night was hard," she let out with a pained laugh.

"Let's go see some stuff and find coffee," I said, both of us aware that the latter took precedence over the former.

I had been to San Francisco twice, but I was hardly familiar with the city. This, however, didn't stop me from pulling the map out on my phone, looking up interesting neighborhoods, researching public transport options, and then speaking with unmerited authority about our plans for the day.

"So we can take this bus to the Castro," I said, showing Miette my phone, "and we can get some breakfast there."

"Yeah, okay!"

"And then we can walk around and find some cool shops or whatever," I continued.

"Sounds good to me," she said with her usual blind faith in me.

We got dressed and headed out to look for the bus that would take us to the Castro, a cultural district where all things LGBTQIA thrive proudly. The sun was bright, and the breeze was cool; the city was giving us a warm welcome. We walked down Market Street, noticing every bizarre character on the sidewalk—the most noteworthy being a man in real live assless chaps—until the smell of coffee drew us inside a little café. The storefront of the restaurant was open so it almost felt like eating outside. We were savoring a gloriously bourgeois breakfast of coffee, crepes, and mimosas and enjoying a breezy conversation when a strange man joined us, uninvited.

"Hello, beautiful ladies," he said with a thick, Italian accent. "How are these two lovely women eating alone?"

Miette laughed nervously with a big homeschooler smile on her face; this would be a test for her. The man quickly noted my raised eyebrow and unenthused expression and left me alone, but he was enamored with Miette's charming giggle and generally sweet demeanor.

"I am Paolo, and you are?" he asked with a cocky smile, looking back and forth at the both of us.

"We," I said flatly, "are enjoying our breakfast."

Paolo, incapable of taking a hint, continued asking Miette questions from his perch on the ledge next to our table with his legs crossed. With every question, he scooted a little closer to her, until he had weaseled her into a full embrace on his lap.

"Paolo, where are your friends? They're probably wondering where you are," I said, looking around at the tables and hoping that this time he would get the message. Miette's face gave away her discomfort, but she didn't know how to deflect his come-ons without making everyone feel awkward.

"I do not worry for my friends because I have my new friends here."

The spectacle, which was at first entertaining, had become overwhelming. Realizing that we had to get rid of Paolo, who was now reminding me of a housefly that I was trying to swat away, we ordered the check.

We followed the hilly streets of San Francisco and admired the graffiti murals and independent shops. As we wandered, I felt cheerful and light; the handmade jewelry, retro bikes, and indie vibes had almost convinced me that San Francisco was my true home. When our purses were heavy with the treasures we had collected, the flowers in our hair had wilted, and our lipstick was creased and faded, we headed back to the hostel.

"What's tomorrow?" Miette asked me from her bunk. The following day was the Fourth of July, and we had planned to meet two friends of mine from Bellingham whom I had met years before studying abroad in Spain and who were now living in Ventura, California. She yawned and nestled her head into her pillow.

"Tomorrow we're visiting Barton and Robin in Ventura. It's like seven hours, I think. But if we want to hang out and celebrate the Fourth of July with them, we should leave pretty early, right? Like six a.m.?"

"Oh, barf. But, yeah, we probably should."

Despite our early start time, I felt anxious and claustrophobic in my bunk. We were in San Francisco! I had never been in the city past the legal drinking age, and in my world, if a person wanted to experience local culture, they went to the bars. Miette was curled up in her blankets and leisurely reviewing her photos from the day. It was clear that she wasn't going to drag herself out of bed and come explore the dark streets of downtown San Francisco with me so I reapplied my lipstick, slapped on my sandals, and said goodnight.

Walking up the sidewalk from the hostel, I noticed how everything was different under the white light of the moon. Had there been that many homeless people earlier in the day? As I climbed the street, searching for a bar to slip into, I approached a man in tattered clothes who was jumping frantically and screaming, "Where is it? Where did you hide it? Where is it?" The veins in his neck were throbbing as he flailed his arms, smacking them against walls and signposts.

He lunged toward me in his fit of rage, his eyes bulging out of his face like a cartoon, and there was an element of fear and desperation to his anger. Startled, I jumped to the side and ran across the street, not bothering to look out for cars. There was honking and yelling, but I just kept going until I saw a chalkboard with drink specials scrawled on it. I heard reggae music and darted inside.

Plopping down on the barstool and dropping my purse on the bar top, I let out a big sigh of relief; I was back in familiar territory. A handsome man with fine, black dreadlocks twisted into a knot on the nape of his neck stood behind the mahogany bar. He glided over and asked me what I'd like to drink. I ordered a Manhattan on the rocks with Bulleit Rye, and he gave me a wink before fixing up my cocktail.

"Whiskey girl, are ya?"

A coy smile snuck across my lips. He took his time crafting my drink and carefully placed it in on a coaster in front of me, leaning in close. Not too close, but definitely closer than was required. This was a man who moved with grace and purpose. He didn't throw bottles around or sling drinks down the bar to draw attention and impress pretty girls. He didn't need to. He understood that less was more. I tilted my glass on the bar top as if I were regarding its contents, when in reality, I was thinking, *And he has dimples? This guy is a god...*

"What have you got going on in San Francisco?" he asked after I told him I was from Seattle.

"My friend and I are driving across the country, and this is just one of our stops." I relished the opportunity to talk about being on the road with Miette. How I loved feeling like I had an interesting story to tell in front of this obviously more cultured, better-traveled and worldly Rasta-haired bartender man.

"And where's your friend?" He flung the bar towel over his shoulder to free up his hands to adjust his hair.

"She's in the hostel sleeping," I said, rolling my eyes dramatically.

"Is the hostel far?"

"Not really. I mean, maybe six blocks?"

"So you aren't meeting anyone here?"

I shook my head and began to wonder why he was asking me all of these questions. And then I had my answer.

"You know, you really shouldn't be walking around alone. San Francisco is pretty during the day, but it has another face at night, and you should be careful. Especially downtown." As he said these words, I felt myself shrinking. "In fact, if I were you, I would head back soon or take a taxi."

Suddenly, I felt less like a fascinating nomad and more like a lost, pathetic little girl. While he had his back to me, changing the music on the laptop, I finished my drink, left eleven dollars on the bar, and slid off of the stool. I thanked him, and as I slinked out the door, he gave me another condescending wink, just in case my ego hadn't been sufficiently deflated.

On my walk back to the hostel, I kept my head down, my hands in my pockets, and avoided eye contact with everyone. When I got to the corner where I had stumbled across the crazy man who had reminded me of Gollum panicking about his lost ring, I felt my stomach clench up, dreading another angry encounter, but this time with a splash of fear. I focused on putting one foot in front of the other, walking more quickly with each step until I arrived at the door, where I realized that I was legitimately scared. That stupid bartender and his sexy dimples had made me feel so inferior and insecure that I was actually afraid that something horrible could happen to me on my walk back, and it's not to say that it couldn't, but those situations never usually got to me. I always thought that if I walked with confidence and didn't wander around backstreets alone, I would be fine. Somehow, in that moment, fear had crept up inside of me, and I resented it and him and the entire situation.

And then I became aware that I was a young woman with no protection nor martial arts training, walking alone at night in a big, unfamiliar city. He might actually have been right. Maybe I wasn't safe. Maybe I was being a naïve child by thinking that I could take on the dark streets of downtown San Francisco alone. That realization brought me to rage. I stomped up the stairs, threw my jewelry and very short denim shorts onto the floor of our room, and flung myself onto the bed, where I brooded until I fell asleep.

I woke up to the entirely unwelcome sound of my alarm going off. In a groggy, pre-dawn fog, Miette and I packed up our things, got dressed, and stumbled down to the car. Why were we leaving so early again? Was it really that big of a deal to get to Ventura so early? When did I even start caring about Fourth of July? It was, after all my idea. Maybe I could retract it as easily as I had suggested it.

When we were all settled in the car and ready to go, Miette started the engine and shifted the car into gear, and she immediately noticed something was off when she pressed the clutch.

"Come on Tercel, baby. What's going on? Do you need your coffee?" she asked jokingly, but the worry was growing as she continued struggling to get the car out of the garage and onto the road. We exchanged nervous glances, but we didn't speak more on the topic, and we eventually made it to the freeway, where the Tercel went seemingly back to normal. I leaned back in my seat and gazed at the Hello Kitty car freshener dancing under the rearview mirror; an image that would become an integral part of the landscape in front of me. The peach-colored sun rising over San Francisco painted the clouds an almost unnatural pink above us, and there was only one thing missing: The Coffee.

We drove for a while, keeping our eyes out for coffee stands, since we were both the breed of Northwesterner that can't put together complete sentences, unless they contain insults and profanities, until there's coffee. Miette and I had laughed on various occasions about how psychosomatic it actually was because the moment that the cup of coffee was resting in our hands, the world made sense again. We pulled off the freeway at the San Jose exit, and after almost reaching our point of desperation, the fourth coffee shop we passed was open.

"It's seven a.m. folks. I need my coffee, rise and shine!" Miette said, pulling into the drive-through, and I laughed, now feeling my newly restored optimism. We ordered two sixteen-ounce coffees and pulled over to enjoy them before sitting on the grass outside the coffee stand.

"I feel like there are a lot of things you have to make compromises about in a relationship," she said, gripping the paper cup between both hands, close to her face, basking in the aroma, "but if one person is a coffee person and the other person doesn't respect, it's just never going to work."

"I for sure agree. I mean, if I have a boyfriend who doesn't drink coffee, which I've had, that's fine, and he may never understand what it is, but he better not make it a problem. Imagine, like, if we're at home one morning, and he wants to leave right away to go do something, and I say, 'Hold on, let me just have a cup of coffee first,' and he rolls his eyes or makes me feel bad, or worse, says, 'Can't you just skip it?' Imagine that. That relationship would be doomed."

We drove with the windows down because the sweet little car didn't have any air conditioning, but the hot desert air was comforting. We had left another city behind us, and we were now driving through a landscape of dry shrubs and rocks, where it really began to feel like we were far from home. I stuck my bare feet out the window and leaned back in my seat, noticing the dirt lines left on the tops of my feet by my flip-flops. The wind was loud, but the music was louder, and at that moment, I felt the simultaneous excitement and tranquility of "the open road" like I had never felt it before.

We discussed stopping for a bathroom and to buy water because we had realized that we were driving through the desert completely unprepared for disaster, but the miles flew by us, and there was no sign of life anywhere. What if the car broke down and nobody stopped to help us? It was nearly a hundred degrees, and we had nothing to eat or drink and nothing to cool the car with if it overheated. We didn't have cell phone service at the time. We hadn't even considered bringing maps because we had those on our phones. But what if our phones ran out of battery? How had none of these possibilities occurred to us?

"Don't they have to warn you if civilization is just going to stop?" I asked, beginning to realize the gravity of the situation.

"You'd think they'd at least have a sign near the last gas station saying there wouldn't be another one in forever."

"If we die out here, we'd deserve it," I said to Miette with my eyes fixed on the horizon, desperate to see the words "Gas Next Right."

"I'm going to die of having to pee. Should we just pull over somewhere?" she asked.

"I mean, I don't know how to pee in a bottle, and there are obviously no bathrooms in all of Central California so..."

Minutes later, we saw a sign for Bradley, California, and despite seeing very little to indicate that Bradley was in fact a town, we pulled off the freeway with a triumphant cheer. Miette wanted to drop off some postcards, and we thought we could also use the bathroom in the post office. Or in a bush behind the post office. We followed the road into a—what was it? There were some houses, some rusty cars parked in driveways, and a post office. But it was definitely not a town.

As we drove, a cloud of dust was lifted up behind us. We stopped the car next to the post office. I got out and stood still for a moment, taking in the Americana scenery around us; there was one straight road that went on for maybe a quarter mile with some small houses along either side, and little dirt roads that went between them. Miette walked over to the post office, and with her hand shading her eyes, she peered into the

28

window. Everything was dark; the lights were off, and I had the instant sensation of being in a ghost town.

"This place is fucking creepy," I said, looking around at the dusty buildings.

"The creepiest." She looked the other way down the road, and then she squinted with her hand shading her eyes. "What's that?"

A beat-up black Cadillac emerged from the dust and came creeping slowly down the street toward us. Where had it come from? There was a man standing on the hood. He was shirtless and wore worn-out jeans. He had scraggly, long hair brushing his shoulders. We were both paralyzed by confusion, fear, and fascination. I couldn't make out the driver, but the stander stared expressionless at us as the car inched by.

We looked at each other to see who would break the silence.

"Let's get the hell out of here," I said, but before I had finished the first word, Miette already had her keys in her hand and was running to the car door. We jumped in; she started up the car, and we sped down the road, this time kicking up so much dust that we couldn't see behind us.

"Oh my God. I have to pee!" she screamed as we raced down the main drag.

"I'm pretty sure our only options are either to pee behind that thing or on the side of the freeway entrance," I said, pointing to the rusty flatbed of a pickup truck that was next to the road attached to absolutely nothing. Knowing that we both wanted to spend as little time as possible in Bradley, Miette continued to the freeway entrance; pulled the car off the road a bit; and with cars flying past us, we squatted, full moon.

We were back on the road, relieved to be out of that place but still a little disturbed by our experience in Bradley.

"So that was one of the weirdest places I've ever been," I said. "Like a scene from a horror movie or something."

"Oh, and that stander guy on the hood of the car. Let's not even talk about how creepy that was," she replied, shaking her head in bewilderment.

29

"Have you talked to Sol at all today?"

"Not today. He's being kind of a dick. Like he's drinking pretty much every day, and he's been getting ornery-drunk lately. Fun-drunk Sol is great, but..."

"Yeah, ornery-drunk is not what you want."

Sol was renting a room in a youth hostel, my image of which, based on Miette's secondhand descriptions, was not a place I would want to spend even a minute of my life. I imagined Miette there alone while Sol was at work. I imagined the fear she'd feel not only having moved across the country, but the culture shock of trading the happy-go-lucky West Coast for the fast-paced and business-minded East Coast. On top of that, she would live in a YMCA hostel with a shared bathroom mainly occupied by men in their late twenties with oxycodone and tequila habits and multiple baby mamas.

It was afternoon, and we were ready to eat something and stretch our legs again. When I saw the freeway exit for Pismo Beach, I smiled at the thought of stopping at a California beach for lunch. It was noticeably hotter than the previous days, and remembering the sublime pleasure of dipping our feet in the ocean at the dunes in Florence, I felt the urge to do it again.

We pulled into the little beach town, and Independence Day was everywhere. There were American flags in every window and printed on T-shirts and even bikinis. The ocean was taunting us from just outside the window as we waited desperately to see the taillights of a car pulling out.

We could taste our relief, but it was just out of our reach. When we finally found our spot, I grabbed my camera and my purse and jumped out, unable to endure another moment in the stuffy car. Upon reaching the beach, we both kicked off our flip-flops and sunk our feet into the velvety sand, seagulls screeching overhead and the smell of barbecue wafting in the breeze. We took some pictures; walked up and down the beach, gawking at the American flag polo shirts and other outrageously festive ensembles; and felt totally at peace with the day.

"We are so lucky we made it here. Do you realize how many

hours we were on that desert road without water and without seeing any gas stations?" Miette said to me as both of us sat in the sand, appreciating all the humanity around us.

"Yeah, new road trip rule: Always keep water in the car."

"So should we go get lunch or keep going?"

"Let's walk around and check out the town a little, and if there's somewhere we want to eat, then we can stop, yeah? And then let's keep heading south. I'm excited to see those guys in Ventura," I responded.

We walked until we found a taco bar and enjoyed some fresh fish tacos. The place had a familiar SoCal-hippie vibe, i.e. our tacos had sunflower seeds sprinkled over the whole wheat tortillas. We finished our lunch, and we walked back up to the car with a spring in our step. In the end, everything had worked out. We hopped in the car, and Miette started her up, only to drive a few blocks and realize that she couldn't shift gears. The Tercel sputtered a bit, and she instinctively eased the car just off the main road.

"Oh my God, Kate. I can't shift. I can't do anything!" she shrieked, right before we heard a loud clunk from somewhere underneath us. She let the car coast into a parking space.

We got out of the car, and Miette immediately got on the phone with her dad, explaining every detail of what had happened, until he came to the conclusion that it was the clutch.

"Oh shit. Oh shit. Miette, do you realize that this is actually a lot worse than it seems?" I looked at her sternly, waiting for her to make the connection. She held my gaze with a blank expression until—

"Oh crap." There it was. She had just realized that it was a holiday, and all the auto shops would be closed.

"What do we do? Should we try calling some mechanics to see if there's someone working today?" I asked, pulling Google up on my phone. I was sitting on the curb, the worst-case scenarios already flooding my mind. Miette was pacing around the car, stopping only to check the brake fluid.

"Or should we walk around and see if there's anyone

around that can help us? I feel panicky. I think we should walk around," she said, still pacing.

After noticing a sign directly in front of us that said, "All Unauthorized Vehicles Will Be Towed," I pulled out my notebook, scribbled out a little note, and left it on the dashboard. *Please don't tow us. We broke down and will be right back! Thank you! Happy 4th of July!* People from the Northwest tend to think that being nice will make everyone else nice. It sometimes works.

We walked in somber silence down the sidewalk for a couple of minutes, and when I looked up, I couldn't believe what was in front of us. An auto shop was open, and people were working on cars on the Fourth of July. I looked up at the sky to give a quick nod to the Universe before we ran toward the door.

After explaining our drama in a frenzied panic, we waited anxiously for the moment of truth.

"Well, girls, it's just a simple question of replacing the clutch. I'd be glad to do it up for ya." As he said this, I let out a big sigh, releasing all of the tension I had been holding inside. "But it all depends on if we got the part you need."

Miette looked over at me, biting her lower lip.

"And if you don't have it?" I asked.

"Well, I'd have to order it, and it'd come in on Monday."

I felt the heavy rock of disappointment in my stomach. Seven miserable minutes passed as Miette and I waited nervously, sitting on the curb, hoping for good news but preparing for the worst.

"You girls are in luck. I've got the clutch you're after. I'll just need a couple hours to finish up these other projects and get your rig taken care of. Bring her on over, and we'll get her set up."

The mechanic was right. We were incredibly lucky. Not only did we not break down in the middle of the desert, but we broke down a block away from the only auto shop within miles of us open on a holiday who happened to have the exact part we needed in stock. My only hope then was that we hadn't used up all of our luck so early in the trip because there was still almost a month of driving left and surely some other emergency would befall us.

We were practically dancing with joy on our way back to the car. The shop was close, but we still had to get the car there, and with a failing clutch, even crossing the street can be a challenge. We got in the car and gave each other a look of encouragement. Miette started the engine, shifted into reverse, and tried to give the car some gas. We slowly began rolling backward, out of the parking space.

"This is not good. This is pants," she said, taking in the fact that the car had completely given up on us. Pants is a word that we had found in a blog post about funny British slang words years before, but we honestly had no idea what it meant or how to use it. We simply used it to replace any given expletive as a kind of chameleonic expression of frustration or disapproval.

"I'm going to have to put the car in neutral and try to let it coast its way there," she said matter-of-factly. "I can't accelerate so we'll have to just let gravity guide us there."

As we rolled into the street without any sort of reliable control over the vehicle, I asked her in my meekest, most hopeless voice, "Miette, are we gonna make it?"

"Well, we're gonna try."

Her no-frills answer struck me as absolutely hilarious. It was true. We were going to try, and that was the only thing we had control over. The two of us laughing hysterically and holding up traffic must have been a ridiculous sight. Eventually, I had to jump out of the car and push from behind with Miette guiding it at the wheel. Suddenly, I had a middle-aged couple next to me, pushing with all of their might, and I noticed some people observing us from the sidewalk with ice cream cones in their hands, cheering us on. Panting, overwhelmed, and losing stamina, we rolled into the parking lot of the auto shop. We tried, and we succeeded. I thanked the couple who had appeared out of nowhere, and we went to talk to our friend Gary.

It was now around one p.m. We left the Tercel in what we were assured to be good hands and went to explore Pismo Beach for a few hours as we waited for the car to be ready. We strolled down the beach barefoot and observed the celebrations. There were tarps set up everywhere, and from above, the beach was a patchwork of bright colors in varying shapes and sizes. In the water, blow-up alligators and unicorns speckled the shoreline. Kaleidoscopic kites danced in the sky, and leathery-skinned moms and dads boogied in their swimsuits with Coronas in their hands, next to their coolers and portable stereos blasting Jimmy Buffet. We were still on the West Coast, relatively close to home, but the culture was noticeably different. Apart from having that sunny, beach-town energy that we weren't familiar with in the Seattle area, I noticed how the general size of the people had changed—they were much bigger—and there were so many visors.

After a leisurely walk and some picture taking, we decided to wander up the road and out of downtown. It was such a beautiful day, a perfect day for margaritas, and continuing our good luck, a Mexican restaurant appeared before us.

We sat down in the wicker chairs on the patio overlooking the beach and ordered the biggest, fruitiest, most tequila-heavy margaritas on the menu. They arrived in glasses as big as fish bowls with plastic flamingos and palm trees stuck in the blended orange ice, making it look like sand. We chatted, twirled our sun-kissed hair, sipped the boozy goodness, and gazed out over the water. I couldn't help wondering what I had done in a previous life to be so lucky. We were definitely making lemonade with those lemons from earlier.

The first margarita was so divine that ordering a second seemed obvious. During my teens and early twenties, I had experienced phases of moderate to heavy drinking and knew more or less how to handle my alcohol, but Miette, on the other hand, was what we would consider a lightweight. She had been quoted on a previous occasion saying, "I'm sorry if I'm a bit tipsy. I've had a teaspoon of wine!" Two cocktails for her was a big deal.

We giggled through our drink, out of the restaurant, and

34

all the way back down the hill until, as they often do after two giant margaritas, the giggles turned to tears. Over the last few hours, Miette and Sol had exchanged some unpleasant text messages, and with our inebriated and tequila-fogged brains, she told me all about it.

By the time we got back to the promenade, Miette was a mess. I sat on a wooden stoop in a parking lot just out of sight from the beach and lit a cigarette. Miette had tears streaming down her face, and my heart felt like it had been turned inside out. Seeing my best friend so lost and scared was like seeing a hurt baby deer and not knowing how to help it. I gave her a cigarette, even though she didn't smoke, and as she inhaled, I could see it immediately calm her shaking, in that strange way that cigarettes give you something neutral to focus on, even if just for a few minutes. She closed her eyes and exhaled, both of us wishing that along with the smoke, her heartbreak would swirl out into the air and be lost forever.

I noticed the air chilling my arms; it was then late evening, and we had left everything but our purses in the car. Our short-shorts and tank tops were not going to keep us warm enough for long, so after another cigarette, we decided to walk back up to the car to get some warmer clothes and ask if the car would be ready soon. As we dragged ourselves back up the hill, my head started throbbing, and my eyelids felt heavy. After all that sugar and tequila, the rollercoaster of emotions, and the few hours of sleep I had gotten the night before, I could feel a crash coming.

We arrived at the auto shop to find the car suspended in the air.

"Fuck," I said, stopping dead in my tracks.
"They haven't even started on ours yet," Miette informed me, after asking the guy how long it would be. "And we can't get our clothes out because the car is quite obviously hanging in the air. Oh, and it won't be ready until tonight at around ten p.m." Our luck was changing.

As we walked back into town with goosebumps creeping up

our arms, the bright colors seemed to fade into shades of gray, and the smiling faces around us had gone cold and expressionless. A cloudy haze had settled over the water, dimming the bright blue sky and giving it a dirty brown hue. As I looked around at the crowds of people, their patriotism was no longer endearing. It now seemed self-indulgent and excessive. Pismo Beach was losing its charm.

We were both shivering, and my clattering teeth chopped up my words. "Miette, I'm wicked cold. I think we might have to buy something to wear if we're gonna be here until dark."

"Man. But I don't *want* to leave more money in stupid Pismo," she said, pouting and stomping her foot.

"I know, me neither. But..." I said, shrugging my shoulders in defeat. "Should we just walk down the boardwalky thing? 'Cause other than the touristy beach shops, I don't know where we'll find anything."

Miette sighed. We were exhausted, hung-over, hungry, and cold. We still had so much day left ahead of us. Getting to Robin and Bart's house in Ventura would take us two and a half hours, and the disappointment of not being able to spend the day with them just threw more coal onto the fire of our quickly growing disdain for Pismo Beach. We shuffled down the boardwalk, poked around various shops, and quickly exited each one after glancing at one or two price tags. We were not paying fifty dollars for a sweatshirt just because it said Quicksilver on it and had a hole in the sleeves for our thumbs.

"I found something, but I don't know if you're gonna like it," I said in the sixth shop we had entered. "There are some sweatshirts over there that look pretty cozy, and they're only nineteen dollars..."

"Oh, perfect," she said with a sigh of relief. I led her to the wall where the sweatshirts were hanging, and her expression changed suddenly to one of utter disenchantment. "Kate. These all say Pismo Beach on them. I don't know if this is going to work." She pushed some hoodies gingerly aside on the hangers to investigate our options, slowly getting used to the idea of paying money for Pismo Beach paraphernalia if it meant being warm and not having to spend fifty dollars on something we hated. We took our time and chose carefully, trying to find the least repulsive option for each of us.

"Now what?" Miette asked outside the shop with the hood of her new Pismo hoodie pulled up over her head. Her sweatshirt was maroon with Pismo Beach written in aggressive black lettering above a design with a skull. Mine was similar but was dark gray with Pismo Beach written in white.

"I don't know. Should we drink? I could drink a beer." I looked out over the water and noticed that the sun had gone down. It would be dark soon.

"I could too. Hair of the dog, right?"

We found a small, out-of-the-way bar with countless craft beers to choose from. We huddled up in a corner and spent the next half hour whining about how awful Pismo Beach was, how miserable we were, and how we couldn't wait to get the hell out of there. I started playing with my phone, looking at the pictures from earlier that day.

"Miette, let's take a selfie," I said, holding up my phone. I messed around a bit more, and then I showed her a little montage I had quickly put together: a before picture of us euphoric and frolicking on the beach and an after picture of us with dark bags under our squinted eyes, hoods up, and the lipstick faded from our frowns. The contrast was enough to send us into a fit of laughter.

We continued to commiserate about how fed up we were with Pismo Beach as we sipped our pints when suddenly someone approached us. It was a man who looked to be in his late twenties. He was wearing nondescript clothes, and there was really nothing remarkable about his appearance. He was accompanied by two other equally unremarkable men.

He asked us how we were doing, a very normal question asked in a very normal way, but it caused us to struggle nervously for a normal response. We had spent the day only speaking to each other, in that strange way that only best friends do, and the sudden thought of talking to an outsider was terrifying. We would have to make complete sentences, use real words, and adhere to normal social etiquette. They outnumbered us; they had us surrounded, and the worst part of all was that they were clearly hitting on us. I couldn't believe that in our current disastrous state, anyone would want to hit on us, nor that after seeing our scowling faces, anyone would even find talking with us appetizing.

It was torturous. They were French-Canadian engineers. They were in Pismo Beach doing some boring research about something neither of us cared about, yet for some reason, we felt obliged to feign interest in. We hadn't been giving any signs of wanting company—quite the contrary. Our general demeanor should have discouraged anyone from approaching us. So why did we feel that we had to in some way play along and answer questions that we didn't feel like answering? To prevent the poor boys from feeling rejected and preserve their self-esteem? Why on earth should we be so empathetic to them when they clearly had no empathy for us and our desire to be left alone? Finally, after suffering through half an hour of conversation, we finished our beers and left, but not before they had begged for our phone numbers and invited us to a party at a friend's apartment. We politely declined and scooted out of there.

From the sidewalk outside the bar, we heard a boom and then a crack and then another boom. The fireworks had started. If I were going to create a real photography piece about this trip, getting a shot of the fireworks on the Fourth of July was paramount. We broke into a trot, which segued into a slow and clumsy run. In our efforts to get to the waterfront in time, my gigantic Nikon D700 smacked me in the stomach with each step.

We got to the water and fireworks lit up the entire sky in a way I'd never seen before. Because of all of the haze that had covered the sky earlier, they looked more like nuclear explosions. They lit up the clouds with deep reds and muddy purples, but it was impossible to make out any individual colors or lights. It was a firework show which fit perfectly with the day we had had: strange, uncomfortable and not at all what we had been expecting. I flicked my camera on and was alarmed to see the battery light blinking. In a frenzied panic to charge it immediately, I ran up the hill through the crowds to find an outlet, again with my camera smacking my stomach. Trembling with anxiety, I spotted a small, family-owned convenience store with the light on.

"Hi, sorry to bother you," I said timidly as I pushed aside the beads hanging from the doorway. "I'm having a little emergency." The elderly woman looked up at me from her crossword puzzle. "Could I possibly borrow an outlet? I just need to charge my camera really quick. I'll buy some gum or something,"

"Sure, hun. There's an outlet over there," she said, pointing across the store.

"Oh my God. Thank you so much. Happy Fourth of July by the way!"

I paced in and out of the shop as my camera charged in the corner behind the Doritos and Lays, glancing up at the sky and worrying that the spectacle would end before I had enough battery to get a shot. Now that I had seen the remarkable way the fireworks illuminated the cloudy sky and how unconventional of a firework show it was, I needed that picture more than anything. It was my only priority.

When a few minutes had gone by and the explosions seemed to be leading up to the grand finale, I grabbed my camera, thanked the woman, and ran out the door. Elbowing my way through the crowds, I reached the dock, hunched down in a squat to get the right angle, and took the one shot that my camera would allow me. It was incredible, and worth every anxiety-filled moment that went into its creation.

Settling down after all of the chaos and hustle, I looked down at my watch and saw that it was ten o'clock. Finally, the Pismo nightmare would end, and we could get the hell out of that place. Our tired legs slowly lugged our heavy bodies back up the hill and out of town to the auto shop.

"Yep, she's all good to go. That'll be five hundred dollars," he told us, and my stomach clenched up as if someone had just punched me. "But you'll have to pay in cash because our credit card swiper doesn't work."

I turned to look at Miette and saw that her face had gone pale. We stepped aside to talk in private. "I can only take out two hundred in a day, and I've already withdrawn money today," I whispered.

"Crap. We have the same bank. I can't take out that much money either," she whispered back. "What are we going to do? I am not sleeping in fucking Pismo Beach."

"Let's just tell him and see if he comes up with some kind of solution. Maybe he will let us try the credit card thingy. Maybe we'll get lucky and it'll work?"

He agreed to try it, so Miette gave him her credit card. He swiped it. We held our breath for a few seconds, and nothing happened. He swiped it again, and again we held our breath, this time crossing our fingers, and nothing happened. Without lifting his head, he glanced up at us with a concerned but determined look in his eyes, and he swiped the card a third time. I had crossed all of my fingers and my toes and was whispering, "Please, please, please" to myself when the most beautiful sound came out of the machine: the receipt was printing.

"Miette, we are free!" I shouted, skipping toward the Tercel. "Pismo is no longer our master!"

"Thank God. I was going to be so pissed if we had to spend more money here on a hostel."

Putting the keys in the ignition and rolling out of that parking lot was liberating, and, putting all of our exhaustion and misery aside, we managed to laugh at how the day had evolved in ways we never could have expected. I snuggled into the seat and pulled up the hood of my Pismo, which was how we would from then on refer to our horrid new sweatshirts.

I felt bad about how late we were arriving to see Barton and Robin, partly because I had been looking forward to spending the day with them and also because I knew that Robin had to work early in the morning. I had met Barton four years before when they had started seeing each other. We met in Salamanca, Spain in a study abroad program over the summer, and I remember the instant impact he made with his boisterous laugh and gigantic, ditzy smile.

On the first night we arrived at Salamanca, a few of us went out for drinks. Most of us were under twenty-one so we couldn't resist the option to sit legally in a bar and consume alcohol because the drinking age in Spain is eighteen. We were all studying Spanish in the university and were anxious to prove to ourselves and each other that we were not among the typical egocentric American tourists who never bother to study a foreign language, although we were quick to realize that the Spanish we were learning in class had nothing to do with the Spanish we needed to communicate with people in colloquial situations, like in bars. I ordered a *vino rojo* which I thought would be understood as red wine, but when the bartender blinked at me, asked a question I didn't understand, and eventually poured some kind of watery rosé, we realized that *vino tinto* were the words I was looking for. How could I believe that I spoke Spanish if I couldn't even order a glass of wine in the color I wanted?

I remember our first conversation vividly. It started with the typical introductions: I study this and do such in my free time, but after a few drinks, the conversation got more interesting.

"So I had my hand like this on the wall, and she was bent over like this," he said, recounting an intimate scene with his new girlfriend, Robin, who was back in Bellingham, "and we were just going at it. And then suddenly there was a knock on the door, and her mom walked in!" Even then, while telling that humiliating story, it was clear that he loved her to pieces. His eyes gave him away.

After returning from Salamanca and meeting Robin, I understood what he had been talking about that whole summer. She was a young woman with a permanent smile on her face and never failed to laugh at Barton's clowning around. I was

41

anxious to see them. We arrived at Robin and Bart's snug, one-bedroom apartment at nearly two in the morning. They had organized a sleeping situation that would be ideal for Robin because she had to wake up early. Robin slept in the bedroom, Barton on the couch, and Miette and I were in sleeping bags in the living room. They were out cold when we arrived, which made the hello-how-have-you-beens awkward and brief. Lying on the floor, I did a quick mental recap of the day. I held my body still, afraid of disturbing the other two bodies that were resting next to me, and I melted into unconsciousness. It was one of those beautiful, effortless sleeps that you only get after an arduous day like that one.

I woke up well-rested but disoriented. It must have been strange for Miette to wake up in a house she'd never seen in daylight alongside a person she'd never met before. I introduced her and Bart for a second time because the introductions the night before didn't really count. I turned my head while stretching out my arms to examine my surroundings. The living room/dining room/kitchen was one rather small room, and the bedroom wasn't much bigger, but the photos on the walls and shelves of family and friends made it sweet and homey.

We took a walk into town to find a spot to have brunch, and Robin was just finishing her morning shift. She was almost through with her clinic hours and on her way to becoming a therapist after years and years of dedication and hard studying. After checking out the town a bit and making our way through the hordes of brunchers, we settled into a restaurant with a little patio to enjoy the California sunshine while we ate.

The restaurant had a Mexican flare, which is probably what inspired me to order *huevos rancheros*. We laughed and shared stories from the last couple years, and as always, Robin and Barton complemented each other like yin and yang and had a childlike familiarity that made them loveable. Barton was the goofy, anti-establishment, die-hard Blink-182 and NOFX fan whose wardrobe consisted of band tees and Vans shoes, and Robin was the hard-working, sensible, happy-go-lucky masters student with a contagious smile. The two of them were reassurance for the rest of us that true love could look a lot like best-friendship and was worth believing in. They talked about their brave move to California, their financial woes, and job stress. They talked about their uncomfortable living situation with their violent neighbor and how they had to call the police every couple of nights because of his loud bangs and shouts that rattled their paper thin walls. As they spoke, there was an optimism in their voices, a sort of untouchable innocence that made me proud to be their friend.

We meandered down the beach after finishing those last and unnecessary coffee refills, enjoying the early-afternoon sun, and then it was time to go. Our plan for the day was pretty open. We just needed to get to Las Vegas, which we expected would take about five hours to drive to. With all of the toils of Pismo Beach behind us, it was comforting to know that the car was in good shape.

Barton's laugh barreled down the street as we made a few last jokes outside their door. "Keep it real, girls. Thanks for the visit," he said, and I chuckled to myself at his skater-boy vernacular. Underneath that first layer of goofiness, a deeply intelligent and sensitive young man could be found. I gave Robin a squeeze, her face practically buried in my chest. I'd been used to towering over my friends since the fifth grade.

"They are the sweetest," Miette said softly as we pulled out of the parking lot. I noted a melancholy hue to the color of her voice. "They just love each other so much." Because I knew her so well, I could feel in my heart that she was thinking about her own relationship. She saw how the two of them were not only surviving an out-of-state move, huge class loads, and their fragile personal economy, but kicking ass and loving every minute of their lives together. I knew in that moment that she was wondering why she and Sol couldn't do the same.

"Everyone is different, Miette. Those two are like relationship superheroes, and we mere mortals can't expect to be like them," I said, trying to cheer her up.

43

The day we would say farewell to the Pacific Ocean had arrived, although neither of us knew how long that farewell would last. That was the beauty of it all. I was saying hello to so many new things without really having to say goodbye to anything. Uncertainty allowed me to experience all of those new places and adventures without feeling obligated to let go of my home. If I had really thought about it, I would have realized how unlikely it was that my adventures would lead me back to where I had started, and I wouldn't have been able to avoid the sentimentality and impending nostalgia that comes with saying goodbye. But, as it were, I was able to live in blissful ignorance.

Nevada

"THANK GOD WE BROUGHT OUR running shoes," I started.

"Because staying in shape is super important when it's one hundred degrees," Miette finished. It was our fifth day into the adventure, and we were already finishing each other's sentences, sarcastic as they might be. Of all the nonsense that we had brought with us, the running shoes were obviously the most ridiculous of all. After all, who on earth embarks on a month-long road trip, planning to drive upward of eight hours a day, and convinces themselves they'll find the time and energy to go for a quick jog through the desert? Probably the same people who bring work and books on the airplane, but instead just end up sobbing through Ryan Gosling films the entire flight.

We drove on through the Mojave Desert, making stops every few hours to take some photos, peruse the gas station snack aisles, and stretch our legs. Shades of sandy brown and burnt green colored the landscape all the way to the horizon, and the smell of toasted earth filled the car. I was getting used to the heat, even starting to like it. When I stretched out my body and felt the sun on my bare arms and legs, I understood reptiles and the hours that they spend soaking up the sun. I could feel my body recharging itself like a battery as my bones warmed up in the sun and the moisture evaporated from my skin. We were driving toward Las Vegas, just south of Death Valley Na-tional Park, and brush strokes of periwinkle and blood orange were painted across the sky as the sun set.

Miette had never been to Vegas before, and as I imagined her in the city of artificial pleasure and twenty-four-hour vices, I couldn't decide if she would love it or hate it. In reality, I wasn't entirely sure if I loved it or hated it.

One of my closest childhood friends, Loriana, had moved from Bellingham to Nevada three years before, and she was working in Planet Hollywood on the Strip. We were going to stay with her in her apartment for a few days and let her show us her new world. Loriana was a beautiful person to whom life had given many excuses for which to lose faith, yet she was the person with the most faith of anyone I knew. When I say faith, I'm referring to faith in people being good, the Universe having a plan, and kindness being the most important virtue. Having been adopted by a Mexican father and a Jewish mother and having an Afro-Cuban bloodline and growing up in a predomi-nantly white town, she was constantly questioning her identity. But in the end, she always did what she thought was right and was always true to herself.

The beautiful dusk light was vanquished by nightfall, and all we could see were the twinkling stars and a few meters of the road ahead of us until we saw something glowing—a mass of white light amidst the complete darkness. We were nearing the city.

"It really is just this huge metropolis in the middle of noth-ing and nowhere, isn't it?" Miette said as she pulled over onto the side of the road. I pulled out my tripod, suddenly inspired to capture her contemplation about Las Vegas.

"I love this," I said, showing her the screen of my camera. She nodded.

As we drove and the lights grew nearer, signs for casinos began popping up along the road. We decided to stop, eat, and try our luck. I had worked nights in a casino as a cocktail wait-ress from when I was eighteen to twenty-one years old, and therefore, I was by no means a foreigner in the land of "just one more spin" and "just one more beer." In fact, walking back into a casino not only felt familiar but strangely nostalgic.

We pulled into the parking lot of a roadside casino and walked inside. It was like a warm-up casino on the way to the city, getting us ready for the intensity of Vegas. I sat down at a slot machine, lit a cigarette, and took a sip of my beer. Pulling out a twenty, I glanced at Miette. Caught up in my trip down memory lane, I had forgotten that she was indeed a foreigner in these lands and that everything around her was completely surreal. Her eyes were the size of the bottom of my pint glass, and she was passing her gaze slowly over her surroundings.

"Are you going to gamble?" My words were almost lost under the dizzying sounds of the slot machines.

"Maybe I'll just watch you..."

I put in the twenty dollar bill and took another drag of my cigarette, and after adjusting my bet to just over the minimum at twenty cents per spin, I pressed the big yellow button. Anticlimactic as usual. I pressed it four more times, watching as my dollars were swallowed up by the machine.

"Let's change the bet. Sometimes that helps," I said, repeating what I had heard so many hundreds of times in the casino where I had worked, although I knew it was all predetermined by algorithms and there was really nothing I could do to change my "luck." I clicked the button with anticipation again and again until thirty cents were all that remained of my twenty dollars. I smacked the cash out button and ripped my ticket out of the machine.

"Fuck this noise. Let's go eat something." Glancing one last time at the thirty cents, I crumpled up the slip in my fist and threw it indignantly at the machine.

I don't know how I could have expected anything different after all of the long nights I'd spent watching the other cocktail waitresses gamble away their tips in minutes. The tips that they had suffered to earn for nine hours calling "Cocktails, beverages...!" in a ribbed corset and miniskirt, hauling ten pint glasses on a tray with one hand, weaving in and out of slot machines and pawing through clouds of smoke with the other.

In that moment of fury, I remembered when I had seen the

coach of the university girls' volleyball team lose her house after a four-month stint at the high rollers' table. I'd also seen an elderly woman who would arrive to the casino every evening to set up her shrine to Buddha and prepare for her gambling shift. She would carefully retrieve her deities and figurines from her purse with her long, bejeweled acrylic nails, and place them around her favorite machine. I'd see her again in the same spot at the beginning of my next shift the following day with five overflowing ashtrays surrounding her and her bloodshot eyes hidden deep in their sockets. I'd even seen a grown woman wet herself because her machine was hot and she couldn't stand giving it up to the vultures surrounding her in order to go to the restroom. I'd later heard a rumor that after the incident she came prepared by wearing an adult diaper. Having witnessed so many lives unravel in the casino, I must have been delusional to expect the casino to treat mine with any sort of propriety.

Now feeling silly about my outburst, I followed Miette over to the restaurant. My bare legs stuck to the booth as I slid in. I grabbed the enormous menu and began scanning the options. It was full of typical American delicacies: nachos, hamburgers, battered-and-fried everything...

"This is a salad? Like a lettuce salad?" Miette said as she eyed the cobb salad in front of her without making any movement toward it. We had ordered it thinking it would be the healthiest option, or at least the most likely to be under five thousand calories.

"I think we're supposed to dip our bread in it?" I said, referring to the puddle of ranch dressing in which the salad was submerged. After picking at and moving around the sad, wilted pieces of iceberg lettuce and demolishing our bread rolls, we paid our tab and made our way around the casino in search of the exit. With no clocks nor windows and everything designed to keep your eyes fixed on the slot machines, it's not difficult to lose your north.

"So was that bill representative of all the bills that we're going to get here? Is this the city of seventeen-dollar salads?"

Miette had never been a big spender, and I suddenly saw how Vegas was going to be a challenge for her.

"I think we're going to have to start preparing ourselves for a few days of overspending and a following two weeks of turkey sandwiches. If we go out, we're probably gonna have to drink a bottle of vodka in Loriana's house to get a buzz going before going to the bars."

Driving toward the Strip, our GPS became redundant. As the buildings grew bigger, brighter, and with more recognizable themes, we knew we were getting closer to Planet Hollywood. We saw King Arthur's majestic castle, the Statue of Liberty standing proudly in front of the New York City skyline, a half-sized but glorious Eiffel Tower, and the iconic fountains of the Bellagio. Around us were people, lights, music, shouting, singing, honking, tires screeching—complete mayhem.

"Holy crap, Kate. I'm trying to stay calm, but this is basically terrifying," said Miette, gripping the wheel tightly.

"Nah, girl. You got this, just stay—" and I was thrown forward into the dashboard, biting a miniscule chunk off of my tongue as Miette slammed on the brakes to avoid hitting a red BMW that had cut us off in the middle of the intersection.

"What the hell?!" I shrieked, repositioning myself in my seat.

"Just breath through it," Miette said, trying to keep her cool as we spotted Planet Hollywood and pulled off the Strip and into the parking garage. We went up and up, around and around, the air getting hotter and wetter and dirtier. When I opened the car door, I didn't find relief, but rather a thick, rancid humidity that made my eyelids stick to themselves as I blinked. We fumbled around the steaming hot concrete playground looking for an entrance to the hotel, and we were shocked when we finally opened the door and went inside.

"I didn't realize we were supposed to bring a jacket to the casino in July," I said. My bare skin was covered in goosebumps and I rubbed my arms to get warm.

"Are we in a refrigerator? Did we accidentally go to the Antarctica hotel?" said Miette.

I had lit a cigarette as we waited for the elevator, and when the doors opened, I walked in with the lit cigarette still between my fingers.

"This is Vegas, girl. You can smoke and drink anywhere as long as it's not a hospital or a school," I responded to Miette's confused expression, which I had caught in the elevator mirror.

The doors slid open, and suddenly we were transported to a different dimension. This was a real casino, not like the podunk version we had seen entering Las Vegas. There were neon lights, cocktail waitresses, people dressed to the nines, and slot machines as far as the eye could see.

"Miette, do you feel a little underdressed?" I whispered, examining my cutoffs, sandals, and loose, off the shoulder tie-dyed shirt.

"Every day of my life, wherever I go, I feel underdressed, so right now I basically feel like Tarzan wandering around Manhattan."

"Wouldn't you be Jane?" I asked.

"Honestly, I feel more like Tarzan. Jane may be a jungle woman, but she's still pretty feminine," she said.

We weaved in and out, ducked under trays of drinks, squeezed between slot machines, and finally found our way to the restaurant where Loriana worked, CaboWabo. We squealed and hugged, and then we set ourselves up at the bar.

"Would you guys like a drink?" Loriana asked, and I wondered how many times a day her lips formed those words. "We have margaritas, piña coladas, daiquiris, anything you want. God, it's so good to see you!" She had always been a very enthusiastic person, and the first phone call I'd make whenever I had good news would be to her. There's no one better in the world to celebrate with than with Loriana.

After examining the cocktail menu, Miette and I slowly looked up at each other.

"Is it normal to order a pitcher of cocktail?" Miette asked me quietly under her breath.

"I don't know. Is it normal that every one of these cocktail names reminds me of the song 'Kokomo' by the Beach Boys?" My finger rested on the Bahama Mama, and I began singing the chorus to Kokomo. Miette laughed. We ordered two margaritas, mine with mango and jalapeños and hers with cactus fruit, and we spent the next forty-five minutes swirling our straws around the cubes of ice, trying to make our fourteen-dollar cocktails last until Loriana finished her shift.

"God, that was a long day. People are so gross. How many times do you think my last table asked for an extra side of sour cream? Six. That is what's wrong with this country." Loriana had been working in the service industry for so long that this rant flowed out of her as naturally as her breath. It had become second nature for her to pick apart her difficult customers and blame the world's problems on people who sit down at the only dirty table or ask for a check split by item at the end of a meal for ten people. And having come from the service industry myself, to me, her complaints were perfectly valid.

"Do you guys want to play some slots before we head back to my place?" she asked.

I scrunched up my nose in a way that told her I had no plans to lose any more money that night. We followed Loriana twenty minutes out of town, swerving, honking, and cutting people off to keep up with her. It felt like a game of *Grand Theft Auto*. Perhaps my memory is exaggerating the scene, and the red car from before had traumatized me and left me sensitive to the Las Vegas traffic, but Loriana had never been the most patient driver.

Cockroaches skittered across the sidewalk, and I squealed. She took us to our room, and we dumped our bags in the corner. When I let the weight of my body fall onto the air mattress that Loriana had prepared for us in the guest room, Miette bounced up into the air. The first few minutes trying to sleep were awkward because each time one of us fidgeted into position, the other was woken up, but we eventually both drifted off. The next day was occupied by laundry, picture editing, and lounging around the apartment until it was time to start getting ready to go out. We had decided that it was the night to explore Las Vegas and give Miette a real casino experience.

As we were getting ready, Loriana took a sip of her vodka 7 and gazed at herself in the bathroom mirror with a contemplative look in her eyes. "Does this lipstick clash with the red in my hair?" She had bleached two big chunks of her black hair on either side of her face and dyed each one a bright, fiery red, which, in fact, was not complemented by the rosy lipstick she had chosen.

"Do you have something darker?" I asked, and she pulled out a tube of nearly black lip gloss. She applied it carefully and gracefully over her lips and turned toward me, waiting for my approval.

"So much better. It's daring, but you look great, girl." The deep purple tone paired well with her tan skin while her thick, expressive eyebrows; nose ring; and red streaks gave her an undeniable edge—all of which was a bit deceiving as she was the sweetest, bounciest, most approachable person I had ever met.

We put the finishing touches on our looks and—a bit tipsy—set off to the Las Vegas Strip. As we walked into the Venetian, I chuckled to myself. Seeing the angels of the Sistine Chapel looking down upon the gigantic escalators was too much for me. What a strange place to exist in the world. My eyes lingered over every person we passed as we strutted our way through the artificial elegance, down toward the bar.

"What does one order in the Venetian? Disaronno? Limoncello?" I wondered aloud, gazing up at the glowing bottles on the golden shelves of the bar.

"I dunno. But I'm getting a blueberry Stoli with soda and a splash of cran," Loriana replied, clearly not letting the extravagant, Italian surroundings influence her ordering.

"Oh. Well, then I'll just get a bourbon and seven. You, Miette?"

"I'll have what Loriana's having. That sounded fun and fruity."

We took our drinks and explored the casino until we found the DaVinci slot machines, which I had played various times in the casino where I had worked in Washington, and which fit the Venetian theme. We lost track of time, each one of us cashing out and meandering to another machine, taking turns watching each other play, ordering drinks, and lighting cigarettes. The small, white baggie of cocaine which I had stuffed in my pocket just before leaving was starting to burn against my skin, so I snuck off to the bathroom to give the night a little spark. When I got back, Miette had won thirty dollars and cashed out, and Loriana was sixty dollars deep. I stood behind the two of them for a few minutes, mesmerized by the flashing lights of Loriana's bonus round, and when I looked up, I saw someone who caught my eye.

He was standing at the glowing, golden bar in the middle of the casino. His glowing, golden hair was pulled back in a low bun, and his bronzed skin radiated sunlight. He was wearing a button-up plaid shirt and khaki-colored shorts. A leather bracelet was tied around his wrist, and on the other a simple gold watch. He exuded casual elegance. I asked the girls if they needed anything, and they declined, still in their DaVinci trance, so I walked over to the bar to get myself another drink. The golden man bun was talking to a few other men who had big rings on their fingers. I didn't see an easy in, so I swirled my drink, took out my camera, and started flipping through the pictures I had taken thus far. Maybe I would appear interesting.

At that moment, one of the seasoned gamblers slid down the bar to ask me if I needed a drink.

"Thanks, but I already have one," I said, raising one eyebrow to the sweaty, middle-aged man hunched over the bar next to me.

"So are you done working for the night then?" his raspy voice inquired to my horror.

"Please tell me you think I'm a cocktail waitress just finishing my shift," I said with a look of disgust on my face.

"We both know that's not true."

"Seriously, guy? Why would I be carrying around a professional camera? No, don't even answer that." I responded to his sleazy smile with a wince, slid off the chair, and weaved my way back to my friends.

"So apparently in Vegas if you sit alone in a short skirt with a drink, you're a prostitute. Is that right, Loriana?"

"Well, I mean, a lot of them are just escorts," she answered distractedly without looking up from her machine.

"Guys, come sit at the bar with me. I want to talk to that cute blond guy, but I don't want any other weirdos trying to buy my body."

The three of us chatted our way up to the golden bar, and the chatting caught on with the people around us. Eventually Man Bun integrated himself into the conversation. The seasoned gamblers from before had gone, and now we were left with Bud Light in a Bottle Guy and Bald Cigar Smoker, with whom Man-Bun had been talking previously. I needed to put a name to the bun. Luckily, my patience paid off when he directed his first words toward me.

"That's a pretty sweet camera."

"Thanks. It does alright."

"Are you like a photographer?"

"I *am* like a photographer. I specialize in documentary photography," I bluffed as documentary photography was still just an interest and not something I actually did. "Would you like me to take your picture?"

"As long as it's not for some kind of casino-freak case study."

I held my camera up, messed around with the settings, focused on his ocean eyes, and took a beautiful portrait of an enchanting man.

"Your tan tells me you've been outside," I said, indicating the mark left on the bridge of his nose and along his temples by his sunglasses.

"Fucking tan lines," he said, rolling his eyes. "You should see the farmer's tan I'm rocking under this shirt."

"Yikes. Farmer's tans are the worse!"

"Yeah, I actually just rafted the Colorado River. Eight days with my family. It was pretty sweet."

"No way! My uncle has a rafting company that does tours there. A ton of my family have gone. I've always wanted to."

The conversation flowed until I realized that Bald Cigar Smoker and Bud Light in the Bottle Guy were gone, and Loriana and Miette were off talking to some straightedge businessman. I began to toss around possible scenarios in my mind. Golden Shane was staying in Caesar's Palace, which was not near the Venetian, and we were definitely not at the point in our getting to know each other to cross Las Vegas alone together, so I had to orchestrate some sort of wing-man situation. I excused myself to talk to the girls while simultaneously imagining him draped in a white toga with grape leaves in his sun-kissed hair.

A short while later, after I had proposed the idea, the whole group of us were walking up the stairs to Club Tao, the Venetian's famous nightclub. When we walked in the door, I could feel the base surging up through the soles of my feet, pulsing up my legs, and expanding my ribcage. Neon lasers flashed across the room and skin slid past skin; it felt like we had opened the door to another dimension.

We squeezed our way around to the bar and got some over-priced drinks, which wasn't an easy mission at all. With my drink safely in my grip, I grabbed Shane's hand and led him to a roped off area that said, "VIP," as I've always been attracted to privilege. I saw tables decorated with expensive bottles of liquor and surrounded by whom I assumed to be rappers, NBA players, and models. When I approached the security guard and flashed him a quick smile, he unhooked the velvet rope and let me by, only to rapidly close it as Shane approached. I looked at him and then nodded in Miette's direction, signaling for him to wait with her for just a few minutes while I had my celebrity moment. After walking unhurriedly around the dimly lit tables and observing the VIP crowd, I slid back through the velvet rope and found my group. Miette and Loriana were talking to their businessman friend from before, and Shane turned casually toward me.

"Did you get any famous phone numbers? Must be nice to be a girl. All you guys have to do is bat your eyelashes, and you get whatever you want." I let his blatantly misogynistic comments slide under my radar because now that I'd had a few more drinks, he was even cuter than before, and I seriously wanted to objectify him.

"It's pretty loud in here," I said, guiding the conversation to where we all knew it would go eventually.

"Yeah, and the DJ is kinda shitty." We exchanged a few more predictable phrases, danced a bit without committing to the music, and he finally decided on the right moment to let those anticipated words slide out of his mouth.

"Should we get outta here?"

I shrugged and nodded, and after I winked at Miette and motioned for her to check her phone for my incoming messages, he led me by the hand through the crowd and out the door. We giggled and stumbled our way down the stairs and back through the casino, all the way to a taxi out front.

"To Caesar's Palace." That was it. I was officially embarking on my first ever one-night stand, and of all places, on the Las Vegas Strip. I quickly punched in a text message to Miette and Loriana, letting them know where we were going, and then dropped my phone in my purse, ready to disconnect from everything that wasn't the Greek God sitting next to me.

We entertained the taxi driver with our charisma, which actually means we drove him crazy with our drunken rambling and sloppy laughter after everything we said, and the next thing I knew, we were in front of Shane's door. Everything happened exactly the way it does in films. After a few hours of passion, I fell asleep in his arms, and everything was perfect.

A while later I stirred, woke up a bit, and noticed something strange on my face, and I lunged out of the bed and scampered to the bathroom. I flicked on the light, and just like in those horror stories your friends tell you in elementary school, there she was, Bloody Mary, looking back at me. The bit of cocaine I had done earlier had given me a nosebleed, and my face was smeared with a scarlet red. I grabbed toilet paper and frantically soaked up the blood before washing my face. Then I was struck with a realization: What if he was also covered in my blood?

I slipped out of the bathroom quietly and grabbed my phone from my purse. Where was the flashlight app? Shit, I had deleted it because I had to make space for some other app. I quickly searched for a new one and started the download. I should have asked him for the Wi-fi password when we arrived; it was taking forever. What if he woke up? Could I pretend it was his blood and that he had gotten the nosebleed? No, absolutely not. I was clearly spiraling. Finally, the app was downloaded. I turned on the flashlight, and—oh my God—the light started blinking on and off like disco lights.

"What's going on? Are you okay?" I heard him mumble in confusion.

"Yeah, just trying to text Loriana to make sure she and Miette got home safe, and then my flashlight went crazy," I improvised, looking up to see his beautifully sculpted and blood-free face. I let out a huge sigh of relief. "And, yeah, they're home safe."

The night had been saved. With my secret safe and my reputation free of tarnish, I went back to sleep, blood-free.

When I opened my eyes to the sun-bathed suite, I was ready to be greeted with a pounding headache and raccoon eyes, but I was happily surprised. Shane popped up, cheerful and bright-eyed—casual sex was a good look on him. He put on a baby-blue, acid-wash T-shirt of a kitten wearing sunglasses, and his golden curls framed his smile and brushed his shoulders. That was it for me—I was in love.

"Did something happen to you last night? There were some paper towels covered in blood in the garbage in the bathroom," he said on our way out the door.

"Oh...um, yeah, I guess I got a bloody nose because—"

"Ahh, from the dry climate. Yeah, that happens to me too. I'm from Atlanta. You're from Seattle. We're not used to the desert." Thank goodness he was an interrupter because nobody knows where my explanation would have led us.

"I gotta meet my family in the Bellagio. They're probably on their way now. We're gonna do something this afternoon. A show or something. Can't remember what," he said.

"I have to find my girlfriends and make sure they didn't get into any more trouble than I did," I said, laughing at myself. We decided to share a cab over to Planet Hollywood where Loriana was working and Miette was waiting for me to have lunch. When the elevator doors opened, we were met by a surprise.

"Shane, there you are! We were just wondering if you had already gotten up... Oh, hi!" said Shane's mom, who was standing in a group with his sister and other various family members.

I walked over as gracefully as I could manage in my short black skirt; sequined top; massive heels; and my shaky, pre-breakfast legs, unstable from the previous hours of massive caloric intake.

"Mom...this is my friend Kate." Thank God he remembered my name. "And this is my sister, Sara." He looked at me and gestured to his sister. She shook my hand, and we all pretended that it wasn't overly obvious that Shane had picked me up in a bar the night before. I wondered if they thought I was a hooker, like the seasoned gambler from the night before had.

"So should we all just share a taxi over to the Strip then?" his sister asked, and suddenly I felt my stomach flip inside out, and my heart started beating in my throat. I glanced up at Shane with desperation in my eyes.

"I think we'll just take our own cab if that's chill." His cool vibes were my saving grace, and he led me outside of the lobby.

"It was nice to meet you!" I gushed through my relief at not having to share a taxi with the family of a man who I had just met and whose body I had so recently ravaged.

We chatted about our plans for the day. He mentioned going to see DJ Tiesto that night, and then he uttered the words that I would obsess over and analyze relentlessly for the rest of my time in Las Vegas.

"Maybe I'll give you a call to see what you're up to."

We said goodbye and I teetered my way up the steps and into Cabo Wabo, where I saw Loriana's face plastered with her sparkly, fake smile and could hear her thanking her customers and telling them to please come back again soon. She was using her work voice which was at least two octaves higher than her normal voice. I plopped down in the booth next to Miette and rested my head on her shoulder.

"Oh my god, Miette. I can't believe last night happened." I began telling her the story, and by the time I got to the part about my impromptu meeting of the family and barely escaping from potentially the most awkward taxi ride in all of history, she was crying tears of laughter.

We spent the day at Loriana's house strewn about the living room—where the air conditioner was—making sure not to put too much effort into anything we did so as not to aggravate our hangovers, which seemed to have set in late and progressed quickly. As the evening closed in, I noticed myself unlocking my phone more and more frequently. I was hoping for a message from Shane, even though I knew it was silly of me to expect him to write me that same day. Wasn't there some kind of three day rule anyway? But did that even apply to one-night stands? Wasn't the entire premise of a one-night stand that you never talk to the other person again, but rather let the memory support itself without the need for follow-ups or post-coitus validation? But if that was the case, why did Shane and I even bother to give each other our numbers?

I tried to remember, as I lay face up like a starfish on the living room carpet, the exact moment when we exchanged numbers, but it was buried between flashing club lights, bass beats, and images of Shane's enormous biceps. I started playing all of our interactions in my head, trying to salvage the fuzzy details that would grow dimmer with each passing minute. The beginning was pretty clear, which was to be expected because it was our most lucid conversation. The club was a bit fuzzy, and the taxi ride was just a blur of giggles and giddy anticipation. I thought about that morning and how we had both woken up in a great mood and there was no awkward tension or uncomfortable small talk. Everything flowed; our energies were perfectly in sync.

I revisited his parting phrase: "Maybe I'll give you a call to see what you're up to." What was I supposed to do with that? Did he mean today? Or was it just common courtesy? I knew with one hundred percent certainty that I wanted him to call me, and that if he didn't, I was going to feel terrible about myself. If he didn't call me, it would be a direct reflection of my worth. If he didn't call me, it would make me exactly what his mom, his sister, and the Seasoned Gambler at the bar thought of me. If he didn't call me, then I was a whore.

I had activated the obsessive and over analytical part of my brain, converting a perfect night into a source of extreme insecurity. What a ridiculous conclusion I had come to. When would I stop thinking of sex as something he got and I gave up? I was the one who initiated the hunt the night before in the first place, yet instead of feeling satisfied and triumphant, I felt insignificant. What was I looking for? Why did I even want him to call? What would we even talk about? Would we discover that we both love mint chocolate chip ice cream, vintage cameras, and the Kills and realize that we were destined to watch the rest of our sunsets together? Or perhaps I just needed validation from him that I am worth more than my body alone, that the connection we felt was real and not just physical, and that there does in fact exist a gray area between a one-night stand and a committed relationship. Either way, I was spinning out.

It was our last night with Loriana, and she wanted to take us out to some of her favorite bars off of the Strip. I went with a more casual look, but I felt like I had really nailed it. I had pulled my blonde side bangs back and pinned them at the crown of my head. I wore a gray tank top, denim shorts, and the black leather and chain link necklace I had bought in San Francisco. I made sure everything was perfect for when Shane called. His calling had gone from a doubt to a possibility to an expectation and had just become a need.

She took us to Fremont street, which is the part of Las Vegas that was often shown in films and music videos when they wanted to depict its glitzy, flashy gambling lifestyle and old-school casino glamor. It definitely had that feel, but when I looked around at the crowds of people, the magic dissipated and the real energy of Las Vegas crept over me: consumerism, addiction, and vices. As if on cue, a step van with pictures of tiny-waisted blonde women in bikinis on the side stopped at the intersection in front of us. Was that a van full of women? My eyes scanned the faces around me and rested on the blank expressions of the go-go dancers. Their gazes were empty, and their movements were mechanical and listless. Feeling inspired by the underbelly of Sin City and its juxtaposition of glamorous streets and hollow faces, I pulled out my camera and snuck a couple of quick shots.

Loriana took us to her favorite drag bar, where the bartenders worked mostly naked in their briefs and the sparkling drag queens sashayed between the dimly lit tables, brushing past the onlookers and occasionally catching one of their feathers in someone's cocktail. I was mostly distracted by having to check my phone every two minutes to see if I had any new messages, only to be disappointed. We had a couple more drinks, gawked a bit at the bartenders, and then headed back to the apartment.

The next morning, while packing my bags, I felt ready to leave. I had never thought of Las Vegas as a place to spend more than two days. Life there was too flashy, hard, and artificial for anything more, at least for me. How Loriana pulled it off was a mystery to me.

The Nevada heat was dizzying, and as we walked down to the car, the black pavement radiated heat and smelled like burning tar. Miette and I stopped at a grocery store to restock the snack cooler on the way out of the city. Wandering down the yogurt aisle, I noticed her expression change, which stopped me in my tracks.

"Miette, are you okay. What's up?"

"Yeah, I just..." She looked at her phone for a moment, and then a big tear rolled down her cheek. "I'm just gonna go wait by the car."

With the bags in my hands, I found her seated on the curb by the car with her head on her knees.

"It's not working, Kate. It's not working. I don't know what I'm going to do. Sol is being such an asshole. I can't handle this. I can't..."

I let go of the bags and let them fall to the ground to wrap my arms around her, ignoring the fact that we were both sticky with sweat and pollution. I felt her shattered and trembling inside my hug.

I remembered their wedding at the Community Grange out in the county four years prior. Miette had looked like a medieval princess in her antique, cream-colored dress and flower-sprinkled hair, and Sol looked like her tall, dark prince. Everything was rustic, and pure, just like the two of them, and there was a sweet feeling of togetherness and innocence throughout the celebration.

How could a union as true as theirs have possibly twisted into this dark thing? As I hugged my friend, I pictured the kind, soft-hearted, gentle-spirited Sol that I knew, and I couldn't understand it. I couldn't understand any of it.

I held her tightly and told her that I had no idea what was going to happen, but that for the next month, I would be there literally twenty-four-seven to hold her hand, sing loudly to the radio, give her cigarettes, make jokes, and drink wine with her through whatever happened. We would get through this to-gether—just like we always had.

Arizona

I BREATHED A SIGH OF RELIEF as we entered Arizona, grateful for the change of scenery, even if it was only represented by a mere line drawn on a map. We had gotten a late start so it was already almost evening when we arrived at the North Rim of the Grand Canyon. We climbed up a road that took us through lush woods that looked down on a body of water reflecting the light of the setting sun. We stopped the car to wander through the trees and noticed that some of them had been charred by a recent fire. It didn't quite feel like the end of the day's journey, so we decided to drive the three and a half hours to the South Rim and find a place to camp.

"Do you remember that night like fifteen years ago when we slept on the lawn at my parents' house and talked about our theories about the stars?" I asked my friend, looking out the window at the night sky.

"Yeah. We decided they were unicorns," she replied.

"When we were little, everything could be explained by mermaids or unicorns."

"And fairies. Magic in general."

The sky was clear, and there was no sign of civilization for miles. The closer I looked into the darkness, the more stars I could see. I had never seen the Milky Way like that before, and I haven't since. Our conversation took an esoteric and existential turn as we contemplated life and death and everything before, after, and in-between. The Milky Way had a way of bringing up the questions "Why are we here?" and "What does it all mean?"

After a few hours, we were getting close to the visitor's center at the South Rim, and we pulled into a gas station so I could buy some rolling papers. It was dark, still, and somber. I opened the car door, and a sickly black cat came running toward me, hissing and giving me its most menacing show of teeth and raised tail. I let out a shriek and scrambled toward Miette. We looked at each other and back at the cat, whose green eyes were electric in the dark. It stopped, and it stared unblinkingly at us. We backed up slowly toward the little shop and quickly closed the door behind us.

As we walked out with my rolling papers in hand, Miette whispered, "I don't feel good about all of these truckerheads." This was our term for truck drivers, the trucks themselves, truck stops, and the general creepiness of it all. I looked around to see four semi trucks, parked along the perimeter of the gas station, with their truckerheads surely resting inside. When we got to the car, the small black cat was poised next to it.

"What the hell is this place, and why is that cat trying to put a curse on us?" Miette squealed as we rushed into the car and gunned it out of the parking lot.

"Holy creepiness. That was a buzzkill," I said once we had driven a bit.

We drove to the visitor's center and realized that, without a reservation, we weren't going to be able to camp anywhere, reminding us again how bad we were at camping. We drove around the park, trying to decide what to do, keeping in mind our limited options. We quickly discarded the idea of going back toward the gas station to car-sleep with all the truckerheads and decided to park the car at an overlook, hoping to go unnoticed by the park rangers.

Miette had anxiety about accidentally driving off a cliff because with the new moon, it was so dark that we could barely see the road in front of us. We parked at the inner edge of a very small lookout, unable to see what we were looking out on, and began setting up our beds by taking off our seatbelts, putting our seats back, and pulling out the blankets.

"I know neither of us really smoke weed, but I just feel like since we have it and since I bought the papers, we should smoke a J here on the edge of the Grand Canyon..." I said, already pulling out the kit. Miette nodded in approval. I withdrew a cigarette from my pack, licked the paper, and opened it to take out some tobacco to mix with the weed my friend had given me for the trip, even though I had assured him that I didn't smoke it anymore. I silently thanked him because he had known me well enough to know that I'd find myself in a moment perfect for getting a little high. I lit the spliff, a joint rolled with tobacco, and passed it over to Miette. We took turns smoking and coughing until the only thing we could do was laugh. We were floating like kites, our abs sore from giggling, when suddenly a loud thump shook the car. I grabbed Miette's arm, and she grabbed the steering wheel.

"The fuck was that?!" I screamed in a whisper.

"Ohmigod, ohmigod. We're going to die."

"Stay still. Don't panic."

"Yeah, try not to breathe. Don't let it smell your fear or sense the life in you."

"Wait, Miette. What do you think that was?!" I turned toward her with an eyebrow raised.

"Wait. What do you think it was?"

"I asked you first."

"I think it might have been a werewolf," she said matter-of-factly.

"Do you? A werewolf?" I said, slightly mockingly. "I was thinking maybe a sheriff or park ranger coming to take our drugs and make us leave."

"Oh. Yeah, well, that would make more sense, I guess. It just seemed really werewolfy to me." In a fit of terrified laughter, we scrambled to roll up the windows and cover ourselves with our blankets.

"I think it's okay," I whispered, peeping out from under my hideout after a few minutes of silence.

"Thank God. I'm way too stoned to try and remember what to do if a werewolf attacks us."

"I don't know if I ever knew what to do if a werewolf attacks us. Hey, so if we make it through the night, don't you think it'd be cool to watch the sunrise?" I suggested.

"Yes! Yes! We should set an alarm. Let's check what time the sun's going to come up." Surprisingly, we had reception, and I set my phone alarm for 5:23 a.m. We snuggled into our seats and forgot about the werewolves and park rangers for just long enough to fall asleep in the wilderness, completely alone, on the edge of the Grand Canyon.

I opened my eyes when I heard Lorde's "Royals" start playing on my phone. The sky was a softer, almost glowing black.

"Miette, the sunrise is here. Look out the window."

"Does weed give you a hangover? I feel like I have a hangover."

"No, but sleeping in the front seat of a car with all the windows closed for four hours does."

We rolled down the windows, which we had closed to protect ourselves from the werewolves, and watched the black turn to periwinkle, which was then lit up by a deep, fiery orange. I stepped out of the car and walked to the edge of the lookout. The cliffs and crevasses began to take shape, and I could see the shadows of the steep canyon walls and a silvery river snaking through the cracks in the landscape. The soft glow of the rising sun took its time waking up the birds until everything was illuminated with the lavender light of dawn. It was brisk, but the chills running over my skin weren't a result of the temperature; I was watching the sun come up over the Grand Canyon. It was a sunrise that the trees and the birds and the coyotes were sharing with us, and I was honored to be part of something so majestic and peaceful. Miette and I were completely alone, not one soul knew where we were, and this was our sunrise. This was between us and Mother Nature.

It was early, but I had woken up smoothly and calmly with a sense of tranquility resting over my body. The crisp morning light of the sun slowly began giving form to the canyon below us and the trees around us, and by six-thirty a.m., we found ourselves in complete daylight.

"No words," I said to Miette, overwhelmed by the sunrise we had just witnessed.

"No words," she replied.

"I bet you can think of one word...."

She looked at me for a few moments before realizing what word I meant: coffee.

"Where do you think the werewolf was last night?" She chuckled, poking fun at herself and looking around the car.

The night before, we had arrived with only the light of the twinkling stars, so we were seeing our surroundings for the first time. We had parked in a small, asphalted overlook next to a small hill with the canyon laid out in front of us. Even with the daylight, we couldn't see any signs of humanity aside from the road leading away from the overlook; we really were completely alone.

"You do realize that it's the full moon when you have to think about werewolf danger, right? So we were actually totally safe," I teased.

We hopped in the car and started investigating the South Rim to see other views of the canyon and hopefully find a little shop or café because we were both in dire need of caffeine after our very short night's sleep. Half an hour later, we came upon what looked like a large visitor's center, some bathrooms, and scattered campsites. We parked the car and scrambled into the building, which turned out to be a restaurant hosting a breakfast buffet. It seemed entirely out of place, but I wasn't complaining. The smell of roasted coffee wafted down the hall, and I was overcome by the satisfaction of having reached our goal.

"I'm sorry, ladies. Breakfast begins at eight o'clock," said a man wearing black. I hated him with every fiber of my body.

"Oh, we just wanted to grab a coffee and go," I responded with all my entitlement.

"Yes, well, the buffet opens at eight o'clock so you'll be able to enjoy your coffee then."

"But the coffee is already made. I can smell it. It's right there," I said, pointing toward the table with two industrial-sized coffee pots.

"And there it will be at eight o'clock."

I looked at Miette, and although she kept quiet, I could see the rage surging in her veins. She squinted her eyes, and she pursed her lips. I resigned from the argument and spun around, muttering profanities under my breath. Outside, we sat down in the dirt and checked the time. It was seven-fifteen.

"That man is the worst. I hate him so much," Miette finally huffed.

"Yeah, I don't even want to talk about it. He's just on his big-man power trip because he's the coffee master. I'll show him who the real coffee master is..." I said, kicking the dirt.

We eventually got bored of brooding and started walking around. The views were spectacular, the air was light and cool, and the sky was clear. The canyon went on for miles, into the distance as far as I could see, painted with pastel reds, blues and lavenders.

There are some places in this world that are just too wild for us I thought to myself. I then remembered the environmentalist Edward Abbey, who wrote extensively about the untamable nature of the American Southwest. I thought of my Uncle Jene, who had always reminded me of a modern-day Edward Abbey. I thought of my dad who had worked as a river guide on the Colorado and had fallen—almost to his death—off of a cliff when he was in his early twenties. I thought of my Uncle Rob, who *had* fallen to his death while on a river trip with our family a few years earlier. I thought of all of the people who had been swallowed by this immense piece of geology, literally lost in the cracks of time. Standing on the edge of the cliff and gazing out over the canyon, I felt like I was paying them and my family my respects.

"Can you imagine falling off one of those cliffs?" I asked Miette. When my dad fell, he shattered a large part of the left side of his body. He lay there—sixty feet below where he had been previously standing, his leg broken and splintered—for hours before he was helicoptered to the hospital, and there he spent months recovering. The doctor told him that the only reason he hadn't died was because he refused to.

"I honestly can't."

I looked down at my watch. "Oh shit. The coffee's ready!" We had both gotten so lost in our introspection over the vastness and immortality of the canyon that we completely forgot about our mortal caffeine addictions.

I glared at the host of the buffet as we walked into the restaurant, and out of the corner of my eye, I saw that Miette was doing the same. We were quite the pair. I knew that her glare was out of sheer misery because her expressions are always a direct reflection of what she's feeling. My glare, however, came from a dark place, a place of wanting to make that man feel awful for what he had done. My glare had malice.

We sat outside on a rock and savored our coffees, whose burnt and bitter taste we masked with plenty of cream and sugar. Now that the world was right and I had my coffee, I was able to laugh about how ridiculous we had been. I had become so indignant about not having coffee that I shot that poor man one of the most merciless evil eyes of my life. When I stopped to think about this for a moment, I realized that we were in the desert and had just expected there to be a twenty-four-hour Starbucks on the edge of the canyon.

We drove down the winding roads out of the canyon and through the Arizona wilderness, enjoying the changing landscapes out the window. It was literally a breath of fresh air, after four overstimulating days in Las Vegas, to be surrounded by nature in all directions.

"Miette, look! A critter!" I threw my arm out the window, pointing at a group of elk grazing near the tree line.

"Woah, what is that?" Slapping her leg in frustration, she continued, "Kate, I seriously have no idea what animal that is!" To try to get a better look, Miette frantically pulled herself closer to the wheel and squinted. I stayed quiet and observed the majestic creatures.

"Seriously, what are they? Are they reindeer? Are reindeer even real? I am so confused about there being actual living animals in my own country that I can't even identify!"

I laughed. "I think they're elk, babe." Miette could tell me the genus and species of any plant I showed her, but I guess animals weren't her forte.

A short while later, I asked Miette to pull over so I could take a picture. There was a small, beat up, white farmhouse in a completely vacant field down a long gravel driveway. It completely captivated me. Who had lived there? How did they pass the time when they were so isolated from civilization? Every once in a while, in my previous life in Bellingham, I would hermit up and not leave my house for days. Then I would realize that forty-eight hours had passed since I had last used my voice to make a sound. I wondered, looking at that farmhouse, if whoever lived there ever went to bed thinking, *Wow, it's been two weeks since I've spoken out loud.*

New Mexico

OUR DESTINATION THAT DAY WAS Albuquerque, New Mexico, which was about a six-hour drive. Just after crossing the border into New Mexico, we stopped at our new favorite service station, which was called Lover's. I had gotten a craving for some popsicles, so I went over to the ice cream case and reached my hand inside to see what flavor I would pull out. While rummaging around inside the chilly cooler, my hands rested on an object that felt different from the rest, and when I pulled it out, I realized that instead of a popsicle, I had a switchblade in my grip.

So many questions flooded my mind, but before I could even start to process them, I had to consult Miette so I shoved the thing in my pocket to examine it more closely in the car, and I went to stand next to her in line. "Changed my mind about the popsicle. The flavors were dumb."

In the car, I reached into my pocket and felt the cold metal in my hand. I pulled it out and snapped it open. The blade was shiny and black and very sharp. I examined it for blood. What if it had been used as a murder weapon? How in the world would a switchblade end up in an ice cream cooler? We talked it over at great length. We were now doing this with everything, even the day-to-day minutiae, given that we had to pass the hours on the road with some sort of conversation. We decided that it was our guardian angel who had left the switchblade, giving us some hope of protection from the crazy world we were trampling around in.

"It's weird, but I actually do feel kinda safer," I told her, running my hands over the blunt side of the knife. "I mean, it is bananas that we've been romping around this whole time like Thelma and Louise, sleeping in our car, and we don't even have pepper spray."

"Yeah, this would have come in handy during that near werewolf attack."

I laughed as I put the knife back in my pocket, and I liked knowing it was there.

We both had high hopes for New Mexico. We wanted to buy turquoise jewelry, eat some quality South Western food, see the red landscape against the blue sky, and visit the ancient Pueblo villages. We wanted to hear the magic of a coyote howling at the moon. We were both jittery with excitement and yet completely exhausted. The miles and the hours passed, and our short night was catching up to us. It was only early afternoon, but sleep was on our tail.

"I don't know how much life I have left in me," Miette said with desperation in her eyes. "And the car is so hot. I'm worried something bad is going to happen."

"Do we need a break? We can pull over and rest somewhere. It'd probably be good for Tercel. It kinda smells like burning rubber and melting plastic in here, and it's gotta be like one hundred and five degrees out there," I answered.

"Yes, I think it's important that we do. Let's stop in the next little town we see and find a place to take a siesta because I am not going to make it to Albuquerque like this. I'm just not."

We pulled off somewhere. We didn't know where because there weren't any signs that we could find. We drove slowly through the dusty and desolate New Mexican town. There was a small park with a rundown playground, one of those old school and dangerous ones that are made completely of metal and that burn your skin on a sunny day. And there were restrooms.

We parked the car, but there was no shade anywhere to be found. There were also no people in sight. It was blistering hot under the three p.m. sun, and we were wilting. Miette and I walked to the restrooms, and when we opened the door, we choked on the putrid smell that flooded our noses. There was graffiti painted all over the walls, and the stall doors were a third of the height of a normal door. The only other place I remembered seeing bathrooms with short stall doors was in downtown Seattle and in some shopping center in Chicago.

"Seriously? There's a children's playground right there, and they need short doors to make sure people aren't shooting heroin?" I coughed out the words, gagging with each breath. "Where are we, Miette? What is this place?"

We got in and out as fast as we could. Arriving at the car, Miette noticed that some liquid was leaking from the engine. "So this is where we die," she said, deadpan. "Good thing you have that knife because we are one hundred percent going to get attacked here."

"This is the most depressing place I have ever been to," I responded, fiddling with the switchblade in my pocket. "Do you think the Universe knew we'd end up here and wanted to make sure we could defend ourselves against the bathroom junkies?"

"I don't know. Probably. But I think I might die of exhaustion and heat stroke before anything even happens."

"Hey, there's a picnic table over there. Why don't you go lie on top of it because the ground is covered with ants and probably scorpions," I said, kicking at an anthill I had just noticed below us. "Rest for a little while, and I'll keep watch."

"Oh my god. I really want to." The poor thing was finishing off her tank of energy. She lay down on the table and I sat down next to her.

"How much money would you pay to be back at the dunes in Florence right now?" I asked her.

"All my diamonds and rubies, man. Every last one."

She let her eyes fall closed and I was now alone with my thoughts, all of the terrible "what-if" scenarios running through my head. What if the car broke down again? What if this time it couldn't be fixed? What if we had to spend the night in Short Stall Doors, New Mexico, and there were no hostels?

What if we had to sleep in the park and take turns on watch with the switchblade? What if one of us actually had to use the switchblade?

I had spent an hour or so battling these thoughts when Miette opened her eyes and sat up. "Is everybody alive?" she croaked. It was time to get back in the car and face the moment of truth.

"Before we try anything, I'm just gonna call my dad and see if he can tell us why there's liquid dripping out of the motor." I waited at the table while Miette chatted with her dad. She was yet again pacing in circles around the car. I saw her expression change from one of worry to one of relief. Hallelujah.

I trotted over and she explained something about heat and condensation, but what I took away from the conversation was that the car was okay, and we were going to get safely out of that creepy New Mexican town.

We powered through the next few hours until we arrived at Albuquerque, where we had reserved two beds in a hostel. It was unclear whether it was Google Maps being a jerk, that the hostel was impossible to find, or if our brains were just melted into soup, but we drove around the same block for ages, looking for the address.

"I'm so tired I'm going to cry," said Miette, her eyes already glassing over.

"Yeah, I don't even know what I need. Food? Sleep? Weed?" I responded.

We finally found the hostel and parked the car out front. It was cute and Southwestern inspired, but that was the last thing we cared about. The only things that mattered to us were beds and no bed bugs. We collapsed onto the bunks. It was hot and a little cramped in the shared room, but it wasn't a picnic table or a car seat so we were not about to complain. It was only early evening, but sleep took over us within moments.

I opened my eyes when the light of dawn crept into the room, and I saw that the other four beds had been filled with sleeping bodies. Normally in a group hostel, you wake up each time the other travelers stumble in and usually ungracefully climb into their squeaking bunks, but last night, I didn't wake up even to go to the bathroom. I looked over and saw Miette's face illuminated by the screen of her phone.

"Pssst! Good morning, sunshine," I whispered. She looked over at me and yawned.

"I slept so hard. I mean *so hard.*"

"Are you as starving as I am?" I started groping around my bed area to find my clothes.

"Definitely. Let's go get some breakfast and see if Albuquerque can make up for the rest of New Mexico that we've seen so far."

We had fair trade coffee and avocado toast in a quirky little café, which did in fact help us feel fonder of New Mexico, but not enough to convince us to stay and amble around the city. On top of that, our driving time for the day was still up in the air because we hadn't decided yet where we were even going. Luckily, it was early. The streets were still almost completely empty so we had time to decide. I remembered that it would be our last chance to get turquoise in New Mexico and suggested that we drive around a couple of blocks before leaving to see if there were any jewelry stores that had turquoise jewelry made by members of the Navajo Nation, whose craft I adored.

We pulled into the parking lot of a small shop that looked promising. It even had a painted wooden sign that said, "Buy Turquoise Jewelry Here" nailed to the shingles. I walked up and tried to pull open the door, but it was locked. Peeking in the window, I saw endless cases of turquoise rings and bracelets, and my heart was filled with desire.

"They ain't there. The owner ain't come yet," called a deep voice from behind us. I turned around and saw an older man, probably in his sixties, fifties if life had been hard on him. He had a big, round gut that was hanging out from under his shirt and casting a shadow over his toothpick legs. He had on a dirty, worn-out cowboy hat.

"Oh, do you know what time he usually comes in?" I asked.

"He should be here in the next forty minutes or so I 'magine. You girls lookin' for turquoise? He got the good stuff."

"Yeah. I mean, it's a must when you pass through New Mexico, isn't it?" I said, laughing.

"Well, I tell ya what. I can give you gals a call when he gets in so you don't have to just wait around. I work right here," he said, pointing to what looked like a small gun store next door.

"Um, yeah, okay. That'd be great. Thanks." I wrote my phone number down on a scrap of paper and gave it to him. I had never been too wary about giving out my phone number to strangers, I figured that's what blocking numbers was for. We took a scenic drive as we waited, and I watched all of the houses as we rolled by, trying to get a glimpse into the neighborhoods of Albuquerque.

"I know that jewelry store was pretty tempting, but how likely do you think it is that the old cowboy is going to call us?" I asked skeptically.

She rolled her eyes and chuckled. "He probably already forgot. He's probably busy shining his guns..."

We decided that it wasn't realistic to continue wasting precious driving time in a place we weren't attached to nor desired to get to know on a deeper level. We needed to get back on the road.

"I think this is Route 66," Miette said over the sounds of the wind flapping bags around in the back seat of the car. I hadn't even thought about Route 66 since we started our trip. I knew it was iconic, and that people crossed oceans to drive it, but it hadn't been important to me.

"I feel like this whole part of the world has Route 66 vibes. I don't know why there's so much hype over that one specific road," I answered. "But I guess it's pretty cool though. I mean, now we can say we did Route 66."

"Do you want to look it up on your phone and see if it is? Maybe we've been accidentally following it this whole time!"

I did as she said and consulted Mr. Google. It turned out that she was right. We had been following Route 66 since Arizona without even realizing it.

"You'd think there'd be signs." She laughed.

"Yeah, there probably were. We were probably just talking about unicorns or something and missed them."

We decided to dedicate the day to making mileage and getting the hell out of New Mexico. It just didn't feel like a place we needed to spend more time. Perhaps it was our expectations that had led us to such grave disappointment, as expectations often do. Perhaps New Mexico was actually a wonderful place, but as it were, we didn't feel any coyote magic nor did we try any Southwestern dishes, and we certainly didn't load our hands up with turquoise rings and bracelets.

My phone rang, and I looked at the screen to see an unknown number.

"Hello?"

"Hi. This is Bill."

"Hi, Bill?"

"From the shop next to the jeweler's."

"Ah, yeah, hi. Did the owner ever show up?"

"Nah. He ain't come in yet. Might've taken the day off. He's kind of a fickle guy. But I was callin' to ask if I could take you out for a nice dinner tonight. I thought I could show you a real nice time."

"Oh, shoot," I said, wide-eyed and bewildered. I looked over at Miette. "We are actually on our way to Texas right now."

"Aw, that's alright. Next time you stop through, gimme me a call. It'd be real nice to see you again. You're a beautiful woman, and I just know I could show you a real nice time"

"Okay, Bill. Thanks. Next time I'm in Albuquerque, I'll definitely let you know. Bye."

Miette was staring at me with intrigue. "What the crap just happened?!"

"He, uh... He asked me to dinner."

My comment was followed by a long pause before Miette uttered the words, "In what holy world?" We were taken over by our trademark uncontrollable laughter.

Texas

IN THEORY, WE WERE GOING to clock in an eleven-hour day of driving because we wanted to make it to Austin, Texas to visit my childhood friend, Lauren. We had slept over twelve hours the night before in Albuquerque so it seemed reasonable, and driving had turned into a neutral, time-passing activity, almost like watching daytime television. But even so, it was going to be a long day. We crossed the border into Texas and cheered, wishing New Mexico a kind-hearted "See ya never!" The energy in the car had changed instantly, just as it had when we crossed the Arizona state line from Nevada.

"Should we sing some cowboy ballads to pass the time?" Miette asked.

"This might be a silly question, but do you know any cowboy ballads?"

Miette broke out into song, one about roping long-horned cattle and which ended in a long string of "yeehaws" and "kai yai yippees".

I stared at her in silence, processing what I had just heard. "Of course you know cowboy ballads," I said, wondering how I had ever doubted it.

We practiced singing together a few times, and then we decided to record ourselves singing. We made a cowboy ballad video with my phone, and then another, until, after four outtakes, we had our perfectly harmonized music video. We had officially gone off the deep end.

"Pull over. We gotta see what the convenience stores in

Texas are like!" I said emphatically. We walked into the gas station and found a big rotisserie of assorted meat and sausages, an entire aisle dedicated to beef jerky, and a cooler filled with Bud Light next to another full of Coors Light.

"I think I have to get a giant jalapeño sausage on a stick because where am I ever going to have the opportunity again?" I said, entranced by the lights of the colossal rotisserie.

"That's perfect because I'm going to need to sample all of the beef jerky flavors," Miette replied.

We went out to the car with our arms full of meat treats and junk food impulse buys when I felt something hit my head. And again. And then my arm.

"What the hell? Do you see the size of these raindrops?" Miette asked, squinting at the sky and looking around her.

"Is that what's happening?" The rain started pouring from the sky almost instantly, dripping down our faces and soaking our clothes. We booked it to the car in complete disbelief.

Putting the keys in the ignition, Miette sighed deeply. "What on earth is going on, Texas? It's like everything is so big here. The trucks are big; the sunflowers are big; the raindrops are big—"

"—the meat is big," I added, laughing and waving around my meat stick as I finished her list.

The drive that day was unending. Some hours were filled with profound conversation, others with lighthearted chit-chat, and the rest passed in silence. An occasional tumbleweed buoyantly made its way across the road before us. We drove through one ghost town after another, each one different but the same: eerie and frozen in time. We stopped the car in one of them to take a look around. As I peered into the windows of the abandoned shops and houses, a melancholy feeling began to creep over me, as if the decrepit, empty houses gave me nostalgia despite my never having lived in them. We walked down the sidewalk of the town's still and vacant main street without exchanging a word. Then I looked up and gasped.

"What the—!" I stopped dead in my tracks. As if the ghost

town weren't creepy enough, right behind the glass in front of us was a skeleton. It turned out to be the window display of an abandoned Halloween store, but for a moment, I thought we were in the presence of a dead human. My heart was beating in my throat. In the display, real spider webs had been spun around the fake cotton ones, and the yellow-colored skeletons were covered in dust. One of the windows was smashed in.

We continued on our journey, and night fell over the Lone Star State. I felt like a lone star in the middle of the wild and rugged West. The road curved, and all that we could see was what was illuminated by our headlights in front of us. We drove for what seemed like hours through the nothingness. When we finally happened upon a gas station, we didn't hesitate to pull in. Rolling up to the gas pumps, I noticed an unusual sound. It was as if someone were throwing Tic-Tacs at the car by the fistful. We were both perplexed by this until we brought the car to a full stop at the pump, and the mystery became clear. There was an enormous grasshopper-looking insect resting between the windshield wipers. Its bug-eyes stared directly at us. And there was another. And another. We were in the middle of a swarm of gigantic bugs that seemed either to fly or jump in completely unpredictable trajectories, smacking into the car, into the walls, and into each other. I was repulsed to my core. I could usually manage to hold it together when confronted by one big bug, but big swarms of small bugs were a grave prob-lem for me. Now imagine those two things combined. It was absolutely apocalyptic.

"Okay, so here comes the million-dollar question," Miette said, breathing deeply in through her nose and letting all the air out slowly through her pursed lips. "Who's going to pump the gas?"

I blinked for a moment. "I mean, I think the only real option we have is rock paper scissors," I responded.

I began mentally preparing myself for either outcome. When we got to "paper," I quickly interjected, "Wait, but is it one shot or best out of three?" We decided on two out of three to prolong the agony. Miette lost, which meant that she had to face the swarm of giant grasshoppers. I felt equally as bad for her as I felt good for myself; we were at that point, after all, almost extensions of one another. I was conflicted but, at the same time, very relieved.

She was wearing a skirt so I took off my sweatpants and told her to put them on underneath so that the bugs didn't find their way into any personal places, and with my pants on, she sat motionless and silent, surely repeating some sort of mantra to rev herself up. Suddenly, during her moment of quiet preparation, a strange impulse came over me, and I reached over and flicked her hard in the face.

"What the hell, man?" she squealed in total bewilderment, throwing her hand up to cup her cheek.

"Miette, that was just to prepare you for what it's going to feel like out there. You're going into the battlefield. You need to have an idea of what you're fighting against," I reasoned.

She kept her gaze on me with her eyebrow raised, and then after a few seconds, she nodded in acceptance of my ridiculous logic. "It's my turn to pay for gas anyway," she said, owning up to the challenge with a newfound confidence in her voice. She opened the door and stepped out into the warzone. I was impressed that she didn't let out even one shriek, but the grimace on her face gave away the true pain she was in. I suffered with her from within the safety of the car, but nothing compared to what she was suffering. After pumping the gas and pulling her credit card back out of the machine, she opened the door and lunged herself into the seat of the car, slamming the door behind her.

She took a moment to recover and then said, "At first I was pissed, but that flick was actually surprisingly accurate." I gave her a slow clap to commend her bravery. Half an hour later, obviously traumatized and still reliving the experience, she said, "Even the bugs here are big."

We were on our way to visit Lauren in Austin, who I hadn't seen in ages. We had spent our elementary school years acting in school plays together and obsessing over Johnny Depp, whereas in middle school we both took a more rebellious approach to things. She never pushed the limits as hard as I did, but she did veer from the mainstream in our school by cutting her hair short, wearing a lot of black, and spending her lunch breaks playing hacky sack with the stoners, misfits, and me. Her grades didn't suffer as mine did and she didn't get expelled like I did, but Lauren's thirteenth birthday party was a scandal. That day we had been hanging out on the bunk beds in one of the cabins at the campground where we were staying and had to scurry around the room with air freshener to cover the pot smell when one of the adult chaperones came toward the door.

I grabbed my phone from the car door nook and sent her a quick text. *I can't believe I'm going to see you for the first time since you moved to Texas!* I wrote.

Lauren had moved to Austin with her family in the middle of high school, which was an earth-shattering experience for both of us. She was still living within her own country's borders, but her stories made me think that she was in another world. There were different rules, different social groups, different economic divides, different ways to prove you were cool, and different types of bullying in Texas. My podunk middle school in the deep county was Sesame Street compared to her first Texas high school.

I was already out of the public school system by the time that Lauren had left, and studying in a crunchy, granola-loving private school geared toward alternative education for alternative kids. Only a few of us wore our hair with its natural color, and a corseted dress over ripped up jeans with army boots was a completely acceptable Tuesday outfit. At Explorations Academy getting high was cool but getting good grades was even cooler so at least in that sense I got straightened out.

We arrived at Lauren's apartment late at night, but she had waited up for us, energetic as always. She greeted us with her boyfriend, whom I had never met before but instantly adored, partly because of his cute southern accent and

83

partly because of his engaging smile. We spent hours catching up on the couch, Lauren cracking us up with her passionate and eloquent rants criticizing society, the government, and anything else that came up.

The next day, she had university classes so we spent the day lounging by the pool in her apartment complex. The water was clean, cold, and crystal blue, and we had the whole pool to ourselves. The hours passed in fifteen-minute blocks—fifteen baking in the sun and fifteen minutes reviving ourselves in the water. It was pure luxury. I uploaded a picture to my ongoing road trip album—the quintessential legs-crossed-by-the-pool-side selfie—and captioned it: "One day I'm sleeping in ants in a junkie park outside of Albuquerque, and the next I'm starring in a James Bond film."

Lauren came home from school and rounded everyone up to get some food and drinks at her favorite barbecue joint. The restaurant was adorable; it was Western themed but with that DIY, backyard, indie flare. The drinks were served in mason jars; the patio was decorated with strings of light bulbs that glowed like fireflies, and the barbecue came with fifteen different choices of sauce. We sat at our picnic tables, laughing hysterically, with barbecue in our teeth and all over our hands and faces. I was already feeling a bit of a buzz from the craft beer sampler we had shared when Trent asked if we should order another.

"We probably should. Miss Lauren here has only had one little shot glass of beer!" I exclaimed, finally noticing that she was sober as a rock.

"Okay, I've got to tell you something," she said, straightening up her posture, "and this is a big deal so you might want to hold on to the table or whatever." Miette and I looked at Lauren, looked at each other, and looked back at her. Trent had a half-smile on his face. She had a glint in her eye. "I'm pregnant."

"What? Are you serious? That's why you're not drinking, you sneaky little minx!" I shouted, taken completely by surprise.

"Yeah, I literally just found out. I mean, nobody knows who isn't sitting at this table."

I lunged over to hug her, almost knocking her petite frame off the bench. We were only twenty-three years old so she was the first of my close friends to get pregnant, and it was still a lot to wrap my mind around. Babies? Moms? We were already having babies and being moms?

"So you're telling me that I haven't seen you in years, I come to visit you, you honor me with the most important news of your life so far, and I'm the first to know? This is the best ever! I am so excited for you!"

"Yeah, I'm kinda freaking out but also stoked in a terrified, going-to-have-a-heart-attack kind of way."

I looked over at Trent. "Mister, are you up for the challenge?" He nodded and laughed. The truth was that he was the prototype of a perfect dad. He was calm, collected, and kind, and he didn't get upset when Lauren would get her feathers all ruffled up about mundane things or started cursing the world because someone mentioned one of her political triggers.

From that point on, our conversation rarely veered off of the topic of Lauren's pregnancy. I interrogated them about how they felt, how they would juggle everything, whether she would take the baby to classes with her, and when they would tell her family. Honestly, I was fascinated by the idea of being a mother, even though I couldn't begin to imagine it for myself. After finishing our dinner, we went back to the apartment. Lauren poured a glass of wine for Miette and me, and we stayed up late, chatting desperately as if it would be the last time we'd see each other.

The next day, we got a late start. We had brunch in a trendy breakfast place, and outside on the sidewalk, we engulfed each other in enormous hugs, for which I had to bend over a couple of feet—as with all of my tiny friends—and we said our goodbyes.

Later in the car, my forehead and chest dripped with sweat as we inched forward on the freeway, stuck among all of the other cars trying to get out of the city. The three feet of air above the cars in front of us was warped, bending with the heat and distorting the freeway before us, and the air was sticky with burnt rubber and car exhaust. Apparently this was so typical of Austin that the people who lived outside the center didn't even bother to go downtown because of the impossible traffic. The city center was a luxury for the affluent and centrally-located to enjoy.

"Babies." I sighed to Miette during our three-hour drive to Houston. "Are we going to start getting wedding invitations from everyone now?" It was a little strange for me to talk like this with Miette, who married her high school sweetheart before she was even old enough to buy alcohol. I was so far from getting married and having babies. In fact, I couldn't even imagine myself in a monogamous relationship.

"I'd have Shane's babies," I laughed, half-joking.

"Those would be some sexy babies!"

"I don't know if 'sexy' and 'babies' really go together, dude."

"You know what I mean. Adorable babies with the DNA to turn into really sexy adults."

"And problematic teenagers!"

I pulled out my phone and impulsively sent Shane a message asking how his weird tan lines were evolving. We had labored for hours over the perfect message to send him in our boredom somewhere between Albuquerque and Austin, and there I was, throwing it all away with an impulse text.

"Oh crap. What did I just do?" I tossed the phone down between my legs in complete disgust with myself.

"Huh?" asked Miette.

"I just sent stupid Shane a stupid message," I said, rolling my eyes at myself.

"What did you say? Were you breezy?"

"I don't know, Miette. I don't want to look at it. I'm sure it wasn't breezy though because any time you try to be breezy, they can literally smell the desperation."

To my surprise, after just a couple of moments, my phone made the new text message sound.

Shane: Haha, my farmer's tan is almost back to normal.

"Miette, he wrote back!" I said. My phone beeped again.

Shane: What trouble have you guys been getting into?

Me: All the good kind. We just left Austin and are heading to Houston. I want to see a real live cowboy.

Shane: If you do, take a picture for me!

"What are you saying? Don't leave me hanging!" Miette said as she tried to look over at my phone while keeping an eye on the road. I started typing again without answering her.

Me: Will you want me to text it to you or show you in person?

I looked at Miette wide-eyed while holding my breath. "I think I just said something that might have been really stupid."

I assumed Shane didn't know that my heart was racing, and my hands were sweaty. But who knows? Maybe his were too, although his eternal nonchalance made me think otherwise.

Shane: Obviously in person, if that's an option.

I quickly recounted the conversation for Miette to get her up-to-date.

"Wait, what? Does that mean he wants to see you again?" she asked.

I wrote the first thing that came to mind.

Me: Be right over ;-)

My phone beeped again.

Shane: Don't torture me like that!

"Miette, give me a reason why I need to go. I have to get out of this conversation while I'm ahead," I said, desperately.

"Ummm, do you have to pump gas? Or something more glamorous...maybe we are going to stop to take some pictures?"

I began to type.

Me: Hey I gotta go, talk soon

"I just kept it simple. Gotta maintain that mystery." I said as I put my phone where I kept it in the door nook.

Our conversation digressed as we drove down the freeway toward Houston. We were an hour away when we saw a roadside jewelry shop just off the freeway and took the exit in hopes that we would finally find our turquoise. The shop was enormous; the walls were lined with glass cases brimming with handmade treasures. We spent the following forty minutes slipping rings on and off our fingers and gazing at our necks adorned with gemstones and silver in the mirrors. After making my studied selections, I bought a silver bracelet with a turquoise stone in the middle, made by a member of one of the local tribes, and a silver ring with an excessively big hunk of turquoise on it. I was euphoric.

Miette didn't buy anything, although I'm sure she would have liked to wear fifty pieces of jewelry out of that store. Maybe it was growing up in the country and living off of the land with her family or perhaps spending her college years in a yurt in the woods with her husband that made her so capable of resisting frivolities, but I did occasionally envy her self-control. I haven't ever been the type to deny myself of luxuries or to spare any expense when dealing with things of beauty.

I was riding on the high of my new purchases as we took off down the freeway. I had my arm out the window and was surfing the wind with my hand, admiring the marvelous turquoise stone against my tanned skin. We were on our way to Houston to see my friend, Steven, who I knew would be a first-class host. In Bellingham, along with the rest of his crew, he had been living in the hotel whose downstairs bar I managed and bartended in. They were all working on a big, high profile project—a barge that was being designed to prevent oil spills—

and he was one of the engineers. He had a clean-cut, southern charm about him. He had straw-colored hair, bright blue eyes, and cheeks that turned rosy after a couple of his famous Hendrick's gin and tonics with a slice of cucumber.

For him and all of the other men working on the barge, the bar was like their living room. They were away from their families for months on end, living in small hotel rooms with nothing but a bed, a TV, and a small refrigerator so the bar became their haven, their kitchen, their meeting point, their workspace, and their second home. They would come down in groups to occupy the stools around the circular bar, with me and the bottles of alcohol in the center. Some of them kept to themselves; others tried to make their existence something important by shouting for shots with names I was always embarrassed to say out loud, and leaving tips so excessive that I had no choice but to learn each respective guy's name, nickname, job title, room number, and special-order appetizers by heart.

Steven was different than the rest of them. His hands weren't calloused; his clothes were tailored and not grease-stained. His fingernails were immaculate, and his facial hair was well-groomed. He wore stylish spectacles and vintage-inspired watches, parted his hair on the left, and ordered craft cocktails with rye, bitters, and elderflower liqueur rather than Kamikaze shots and pints of Bud Light. He spoke with a slight Southern drawl, but only when pronouncing certain words, and his colloquial use of "y'all" was effortless and entirely contagious. Oh, and he danced and partied like a maniac, which I had learned after running into him in the famous gay bar, Rumors Cabaret in downtown Bellingham.

I had always imagined that it must have been a struggle for him to be around all of his boisterous, rough-and-tumble co-workers, when he was such a collected and mature person. On top of that, many of them were also clearly uncomfortable with homosexuality. They were the typical macho-men that would spend their evenings pounding beers and arguing fiercely over sports-related banalities in a constant battle to prove their heterosexuality to each other, to themselves, or maybe even to Steven.

"You're going to love Steven," I said to Miette as we sped down the freeway. With my arm still out the window, a sudden gust of wind hit my hand at just the right angle with just enough force to send my new ring flying off my finger and into the dried grass and shrubs along the road.

"Oh my God! My ring!" I yelled over the music and wind.

"Oh no!" Miette shrieked back, automatically braking and skidding the car to a stop on the shoulder after taking a quick glance to ensure that there was no one behind us. We were on the very narrow shoulder of the freeway, precariously parked and absolutely in danger, hustling to get out and start rummaging through the grass for my ring. We were an absurd sight to see. The both of us were hunched over, combing the grass as the semi-trucks whizzed by, each one honking to express their concern and frustration over our dangerously positioned car.

After fifteen minutes, I started clomping my way through the grass and back to the car with my hands in my pockets.

"Did you find it?" she yelled over the thunderous passing of the semis.

"No. I let it go."

Back in the car, Miette was somber. "I'm so sorry, hun. You must be so upset. What was the Universe thinking back there?"

"Teaching me a lesson on attachment." I surprised myself with how calmly I was reacting to the sudden loss and the fact that my reaction was completely authentic. I wasn't holding back tears nor putting on a strong face. I was actually okay with leaving my beautiful, new, turquoise treasure that I had been searching for over the last week and had just spent a chunk of my precious savings on in the dirt on the side of the freeway somewhere between Austin and Houston. In the scheme of things, it was an entirely non-consequential event, although hugely disappointing. I felt a small life lesson wash over me, a sort of understanding of something much bigger that had nothing to do with a ring or any other material possession. Sometimes we just have to accept when something isn't meant for us, even if we think we love it or possibly even need it. Perhaps especially if we think we need it.

When we arrived at Houston, it was early evening, and Steven was waiting outside his duplex in the outskirts of the city. As we pulled in, I could see him waving and smiling before he rushed over to greet us and help us with our backpacks. I hopped out of the car and sprung up to wrap my arms around his neck, giving him a warm, unbridled hug. He looked completely in his element back in his home state and in his own house instead of in a small port town in Washington in a midrange hotel. His house was exactly what Steven's house should be: tidy, trendy, tasteful, and absolutely functional. We had our own little room downstairs where we fluffed out our sleeping bags and felt perfectly at home.

His friend Levi came over, and Steven rallied all of us into his Jeep Wrangler. Miette and I climbed into the back, and the two boys sat in the front. It was the golden hour so everything was glowing in the magical evening light. Steven put on "Pumped up Kicks" by Foster the People, and we sang at the top of our lungs. We were young; we were cool, and we were happy. Nothing could touch us as we cruised along.

Steven first impressed us with his gastronomical savvy by taking us to a taco bar, where no combination of vegetables, meat, cheese and salsa was left unexplored. Next, he took us to a bar called Art Nouveau. I opened the door, and my eyes filled with wonder. We were standing in a big room with black walls and dark wooden floors, and mosaicked glass lamps hung from the ceiling. It felt like a scene from *Aladdin*. We sat at a table amidst the soft, colorful glow, sipping white wine and talking about the unpredictability of life.

The sun had set, and we stepped out of the bar into dusk. Steven drove us through downtown, where the buildings were tall and shiny, their sides like mirrors reflecting the lights of the city. We then found ourselves in a bar that had that local-watering-hole feel. At this point, I was feeling a little tipsy after the beer and two glasses of wine I had drunk. I looked over at Miette; she was already giggling in a way that let me know that she was one step beyond tipsy. I glanced at Steven and saw his rosy cheeks, a sure sign that he was having as good a time as we were. That was it; we were committed to the night. From that point on, anything could happen. And in my experience, when anything can happen, it usually does.

In the taxi on our way to F Bar, I was laughing so hard that my cheeks hurt. We were on a euphoric drive to Houston's most renowned gay bar to watch two famous twin strippers do whatever strippers do. I had only ever been to one strip club in Vancouver, Canada years ago, where the dancer was dressed up in fringe and she stomped around the stage like a My Little Pony. Miette, naturally, was about to have her first stripper experience.

After waiting ages in line outside the club, the security guard opened up the door to let us into the world of mayhem. The music rattled my rib cage while I squeezed my way through the crowd to get a look at the performers. As I squinted over the top of the sea of heads surrounding me, I was blinded every few seconds by a sweeping spotlight. I noticed an extravagant crystal chandelier in the middle of the ceiling, some shiny couches and lounge chairs, and a glint of sparkle on every surface. We sloshed our bright pink martinis around as we danced to "It's Raining Men." During the song, beautiful men in sexy yellow raincoats stood under showers of water falling from the ceiling. The air was humid and smelled of hot, sweaty bodies and rancid cologne.

I braced myself against Steven as we fumbled our way out of the club hours later and into the crisp night. I took a huge gulp of the fresh two a.m. air, as if it were a glass of cold water. Miette's hair was plastered to her forehead. Levi wasn't ready to leave the party and he kept dancing to the echoes of music from the club and the blinking blue-and-red lights of the cop cars around us, as if they were strobe lights. Between the sweaty selfies we had to take and the words we exchanged with other drunk people, we entertained ourselves for about a half hour Steven eventually got on the phone to call a taxi, which took an eternity, but it eventually delivered us safely home.

Back at Steven's duplex, Levi and I got into a profound, drunken 4:00 a.m. conversation while lying on the slanted cement driveway and gazing up at the stars. He told me about the girl who had most recently broken his heart, but I didn't hear a quiver of heartbreak in his voice. Throughout the night, I had been silently building a case against Levi's heterosexuality, as if I had any right to analyze people in order to tell them who they were. I had even flirted with him, shamelessly touching his arm and making penetrating eye contact. After receiving no recognition, I decided without a doubt that he was gay and in the closet. It was an incredibly vain conclusion to come to, but that was how my alcohol-soaked brain was processing the external stimuli of that night. It was fortunate that most of the booze had worn off by the time we were lying on the driveway because otherwise nothing would have held me back from trying to kiss him in an attempt to force him out of the closet.

The next morning, after a little tap on the door, Miette and I opened our sleep-encrusted eyes to see Steven's sharp nose and dazzling baby blues peek into the room. With spatula in hand and in the most lazy, Southern twang that I had ever heard, he asked, "How y'all like y'all's eggs?"

"What a stinkin' cutie!" Miette said after Steven had gone upstairs as she rummaged around on the floor in her sea of clothes and pillows. I was still laughing at the classic southern hospitality that we had just enjoyed.

"Alright, princess." I shaped the words through a big yawn while stretching my arms toward the ceiling. "Let's see what we can do about these hangovers."

Our perfectly scrambled eggs were waiting for us upstairs on the kitchen counter next to steaming cups of coffee. "Levi gone?" I asked Steven, remembering our big talk just a few hours earlier.

"Yeah, he took off last night. Did you have fun?"

"Are you kidding? I had a frickin' blast," I said, picking up my cup of coffee. "Yesterday was awesome, think about how yesterday morning I was having a nice breakfast with Lauren in Austin, and later the same day I was raging it up with my boy, Steve, in downtown Houston."

"We're moving so fast it makes it seem like a ton of time has gone by," said Miette. "It's only been ten days since we left, but my brain is already thinking that first night camping at Beverly Beach was weeks ago."

After we had finished eating, Steven collected our dishes. "If you ladies want to take a shower and then go see a couple of things around Houston, I know some places nearby that I think you'll like."

"Steven, honestly, after what I've seen, I trust you with all the choices about all the plans, food, and fashion for the rest of my life," Miette responded, sliding off the barstool.

He took us to a park where we saw an austere brown-gray cement building tucked among some trees and behind a still pool of water.

"This is the Rothko Chapel," he explained. "It's a non-denominational center for prayer and meditation that was named after the abstract artist Mark Rothko."

"Steven, I say this with all the respect in my heart, but before coming here and going to gay bars and non-denominational chapels, I thought Houston was just cowboys, homophobes, and Angus steaks," I said and laughed.

We walked softly into the empty chapel and let the peace loosen our joints and wash over our minds. I leafed through some of the different religious texts that were on a stand in the front. We each sat down on a different wooden bench and steeped in the tranquility of the room. Without exchanging a word, we remained in stillness for fifteen minutes until somehow, as if energetically connected, we gently stood up together and peacefully found our way back into the park.

"That was beautiful." Miette sighed. Steven and I both nodded and smiled.

Next, he took us to the Houston Center for Photography. My eyes rested on and took in every image on the white walls, feeling every nuance and appreciating every crop, every focal point, and every composition. In the end, I was savoring each and every moment of a perfect morning in a city I didn't even expect to enjoy. I had been served yet another lesson on expectations.

We finished our tour of the exhibitions and walked outside, where we stood in the grass outside of the photography center preparing for the inevitable goodbyes. I felt a little twinge in my heart. After being so exquisitely comfortable and feeling so at ease with my company, I was sad to leave. Steven had been our last visit of the trip as well as our last planned stop because I had no friends in the Southeast or on the East Coast, nor had I made any hostel reservations. We would now enter into the second phase of our journey and into completely uncharted territory. It felt almost like letting go a second time. After letting go of Bellingham and then letting go of the Pacific Ocean, we were now letting go of every familiar face we knew.

Louisiana

"HOW'S SOL?" I ASKED MIETTE as we charged down the I-10 east. It had been a while since we had talked about her marital situation, which I was hoping meant that it had calmed down since her breakdown in the parking lot in Las Vegas.

"He's drinking a lot of Jagermeister," she said as if that would summarize everything.

"Okay...I'm not entirely sure what that means."

"Well, I feel like every time I talk to him, he's either just got home, cranky and tired from work and pulling out the Jager, or he's been home for a while and is now drunk and petulant because of all the Jager. So it's just always Jager."

"Well, shoot. So you guys are just going to live in that youth hostel? Aren't those divided by gender or something?"

"Kate, I don't know!" Her voice became shrill and desperate. "There's a communal shower. Am I supposed to just go shower with all these weird guys? And honestly, it doesn't seem very safe. Like, I don't know this place. It sounds kind of like ass New Jersey, and all of the guys he talks about take drugs and have two or three baby mamas."

I began picturing Sol drinking Jager with some guy doped up on Oxycontin, talking about his psycho ex-wife, who was shaking him down for child support. It didn't fit. Sol was a sweet, goofy, earthchild as far as I knew, and this new world he had entered into didn't make sense to me.

"One day at a time, girl. Hopefully this is just a weird phase.

Keep in mind that he's alone, on the other side of the country, fighting with his wife and learning how to do a completely new job. That being said, he could go ahead and stop being a jerk about it."

The miles flew by, and we cheered, as we always did, when we crossed the border into Louisiana. We were now in the deep South, a part of the world that I had only ever seen in movies. We passed through the city of Lafayette, and as we traveled deeper into Louisiana, the landscape became lusher and greener.

"Can you believe these swamplands? I'd kill to spend a week in the lab running tests on all of these plant species," Miette said, barely concentrating on the road. "I mean, just look at this biosphere. It's so cool!"

"I didn't realize you were so passionate about swamps," I said, skeptical yet amused.

"Are you kidding? My dream job would be to hang out in swamps all day and study the plants."

We had pulled off of the freeway after seeing signs for the Atchafalaya National Wildlife Refuge, thinking that we could at least get a taste of some Louisiana marshlands, even if we didn't go all the way into the park. In all of my travels, I had never seen such a landscape. Everything was soggy and still. The soppy, algae-covered ground was the same color as the green tree canopy above, and I wasn't even sure if the ground was ground or if it was a body of water. Miette spewed out a few facts about marshland vegetation, and then she pulled out her phone to do some plant genus investigation.

"Remember somewhere in Nevada when we were talking about how we needed trail names?" I asked. "And remember how we said those things just kind of happened naturally and couldn't be forced?"

"Yeah," she answered distractedly without lifting her gaze up from her Google image search.

"Your nickname is Swamps—Mama Swamps."

At that moment, she raised her head slowly with a little

sparkle in her eyes, and she said, "Yes. And you—you are Baby Dunes."

We continued along our course toward Baton Rouge, where we decided that New Orleans was where we would sleep that night. In my searching for hostels, I was never one to study the options too carefully. We had a car to get to wherever it was we needed to go; we were used to discomfort, and as long as there were beds and a bathroom, we would be set. I did, generally, try to keep us out of very central areas. We liked to walk, and the closer you are to central downtown, the more shenanigans you find yourself in. I was more of a backstreets and barrios kind of traveler.

"All right, Swamps. We've got two nights in New Orleans."

"New Orleans is gonna be amazing."

"Oh shit. Look at this bridge! Miette, I think we are about to cross the Mississippi River!"

"No way! This is a big deal. The frickin' Mississippi!"

We drove the 4.3 miles over the metal bridge known as the Horace Wilkinson and into the city of Baton Rouge. We stopped to stretch our legs and walk along the monstrous river, feeling the hot wind stick to our faces. We hopped back in the car and took a scenic drive around the neighborhoods. We were driving through some backstreets when I looked up and saw the street sign for W. Garfield.

"Miette, I know this street. Why do I know this street?" We drove past a little turquoise house with the numbers "1330" hanging crooked above the door, a beat up American flag stuck in an empty flower pot, a hula hoop hanging from the dingy pink shutters, and a strange shrine to Michael Jackson on the wall next to the door.

"I feel like this is some kind of iconic ghetto. Like there was some rapper from here, but I don't remember who." I pulled out my phone and typed in "rapper, Baton Rouge, W. Garfield."

"Did anything come up?" Miette asked.

"Oh, that's right. That kid Lil Boosie! I have no idea how I knew that, but here, let me read you the Wiki page." We learned from the internet that W. Garfield was a notorious street on the South Side, infamous for crime and drug trafficking, and that the rapper Lil Boosie was born there.

"Hm. I don't feel in danger here," Miette said thoughtfully, "but the internet sure wants us to think we are."

"That's the thing about media. Yeah, if we were stupid and drove around at night looking like scared teeny boppers, I'm sure we could easily get carjacked. But it's six p.m., and there is absolutely no one on the street."

We GPSed our way back onto the freeway and continued on for another two hours, crawling through traffic into New Orleans. The city was buzzing with people in the streets, and just as the sun was setting, we navigated our way to our hostel, perfectly located about ten blocks outside the madness. We locked up our valuables in the hostel safe box, and we took off to explore. Flip-flopping in our sandals down the sidewalk, I could feel the sweat dripping down my chest. It was dark out, but it was still suffocatingly hot. Suddenly, something smacked onto the ground in front of us, and we both jumped. It scattered off the sidewalk and into the street.

"Nooooooo!" Miette screamed, scooting backward while her eyes darted around us.

"Was that a rat? Did a rat just fall from the tree?"

"No." She shook her head solemnly. "I think it was a tree bug. And now we can't walk under any trees ever again in this city." Another one scampered across the sidewalk, and we saw clearly that it was a colossal red cockroach.

We wandered our way toward the French Quarter and found ourselves on Bourbon Street, New Orleans's iconic street for live music, drinks on balconies, drinks in the street, and more drinks anywhere else you desire. Hordes of people made their way toward the bars, singing, stumbling, and splashing beer on themselves. Mardi Gras beads and empty plastic cups were scattered on the ground. Three alert cops on horseback trotted around the main entrance, scanning the masses for misconduct. We dipped into a bar and ordered some fried okra, hush puppies, and fried pickles because we had only grazed on grapes and carrots from the cooler since our breakfast at Steven's house.

The farther we walked down the street, the faster my amusement wore off. In the end, we were just being channeled down a main street with hundreds of embarrassing drunk tourists, just like on any other well-known street in any other famous city. I nudged Miette down a side street. "I gotta get off this road, man. It's grossing me out."

"Oh, thank god!" I don't know how we did it, but we always managed to be on the same page about everything.

We zig-zagged through the French Quarter and found ourselves on a dark backstreet with storefronts that said things like "Palm Reader, Bring Your Past to Meet Your Future" and "Alchemy Revolution," We stepped through the creaky door into one of the shops to find ourselves in a small, dimly-lit room cluttered with amulets, deities, altars, and other magical objects. Against one wall was a large, dusty mirror on a dark wooden desk, which was covered with skulls of different sizes, candles, and incense. Directly in front of the mirror was a black pot full of small scraps of paper with messages people had written to their deceased loved ones because this was an altar of the dead. There were also unsmoked cigarettes strewn about the desk left as offerings. I gingerly picked up different objects from the shelves around the shop to inspect each one's secrets. There was a basket of crystals, each with different purposes and properties, and we spent some time finding the crystal that most resonated with us at the moment. I left with a small white opal, which promised me creativity, energy, inner fire, and enthusiasm.

We continued making our way down winding alleys, and I noticed that the streets were growing even darker, more sparsely populated, and that the energy around us was changing. Various clusters of four or five people whispering together hid in dark corners of the alleys, and other individuals walked by swiftly with a look of intent in their eyes. I felt as if I had taken a wrong turn and had found myself in Harry Potter's Knockturn Alley.

In one corner, faintly illuminated by a small streetlight, were five figures, all dressed in black and huddled together so that none of their faces could be seen through the shadows. My gaze rested on them as I was overcome with suspicion and intrigue. Suddenly, one of the hooded figures flicked his head in a quick, serpentine motion, and his eyes locked onto mine. I felt an instant chill come over my body, and my breathing was paralyzed. His eyes were solid black, with no pupils nor whites. Only a moment passed, but those black orbs penetrated my entire being with darkness and sent a rush of terror pulsing through my veins. As quickly as he had turned his head to look at me, he lizard-flicked it back into the huddle, and his pale face disappeared into the shadows. I could hardly move, but I managed to glance at Miette and see an expression of terror on her face.

"Start fucking walking as fast as you fucking can in any direction right now," I whispered to her, and we took off, not quite running so as not to draw too much attention to ourselves, but getting far away from the lizard-man and his black orbs of death as quickly as possible. We walked and walked in horrified silence and without stopping to look at street signs or our GPS. As if guided by intuition or some greater force, we found ourselves back on the familiar streets near our hostel fifteen minutes later. Without consulting Miette, I directed my steps toward a small tavern, where I sat down at the bar and ordered a shot of whiskey.

"Me too," said Miette. I was surprised because whiskey was usually too strong for her taste.

"We're going to need to talk about what just happened." I twirled my empty shot glass on the bar top, but I didn't look up to make eye contact as I spoke.

"Kate, I have a yucky feeling inside."

"Yeah..."

"Like really yucky."

"Yeah..."

"Um, like, I have the feeling of just having seen the devil."

"Yeah."

It took us a couple more shots of Maker's Mark to really begin to shake off the sinister energy that had come over us. Eventually, we managed to laugh about it awkwardly, but we both knew that although the whole ordeal had passed in a fraction of a second, the image of those two glossy black eyes had been seared into our memories and would never completely fade away.

We trudged our way back to the hostel, still rattled but now also a bit drunk. I noticed myself glancing in the dark corners expecting to make out Halloween-like shapes in the shadows. "You gonna have nightmares?" I asked Miette as we walked up the steps to the hostel.

"For the rest of my life."

I woke up the next morning sweaty and hot in my small bunk, which was one of eight in the room we were sharing. We got our things together and went out to the car, noticing the high humidity in the air. We had discussed the night before going to a palm reader or fortune teller because New Orleans was definitely a city known for its psychic energy. After nearly crossing into the Underworld the night before, we knew it was a place where strange and mystical things could happen.

We found a fortune-telling studio where we could have our tea leaves read on our way out of the city. It was called Bottom of the Cup and had been a landmark in New Orleans since 1929. I sat in the tea room, gazing at the shelves of crystals and tarot cards, while we waited for the psychic, who eventually came out and beckoned for me to follow her back into the reading room. It was dark, musty, and overcrowded with the same magical paraphernalia that we had been looking at in the shop the night before. She turned on a large recorder with a CD inside, and then she explained how I should drink the tea, flip the cup, rest my hand over it to give it my vibrations, and then spin the handle three times counter-clockwise. She then examined the tea leaves that were left in the cup for just a moment before she began speaking.

"I see you are embarking on a new adventure. I see a lot of learning in your future, but not in a classroom environment. In the future, you will have the opportunity to draw upon things you already know and deepen your understanding of your practice, but further education will not be required."

I sat quietly for a moment. Was she talking about my recently returning to photography? I had been suffering doubts about what to do after the road trip was over. Would I get out of the car in Boston and apply to their photography school, which I had visited earlier in the year? Or would shelling out all of that money after I had already finished my four-year degree in a completely unrelated discipline be a frivolous waste of time? I didn't know if going back to school for photography would be necessary, or if I could learn everything on my own. What the psychic was saying was making a lot of sense to me.

"You're not in love, and you haven't been for a while. You're not looking for love, but rather for a fire to awaken something within your spirit, but what you don't know is that love is going to find you anyways, and it's going to be soon. In fact, I think the big love of your life might be surprisingly close to finding you."

"So it's not someone I already know?" I asked while all my different exes and recent flings spun like a slot machine through my mind and eventually landed on Shane's sweet, dimpled face.

"No. This will be someone new. Someone close, but far away."

"Oh. Well, I guess if I have to fall in love, I'll fall in love. But, yeah, totally not out there on the hunt right now."

"So before we finish, did you have any specific questions for me?"

I pondered her words for a moment. I was riddled with questions, but I didn't know how specific I could make them.

"What's on your mind more than anything else lately?" she asked.

"Okay. Well, where am I going? Where am I supposed to end up?"

"The end of this trip won't be the end of your travels. There is another big journey that you will undertake." Her calm and confident voice made me forget that I hadn't so much as alluded to the trip we were on. She then carefully took the CD out of the machine, scribbled some words on it, and handed it to me in an envelope.

"We record the sessions so that you can refer back to them in the future," she said, standing up and opening the curtain. I walked back out to the main room and raised my eyebrows at Miette, a gesture assuring her that New Orleans was indeed full of magic. She came out fifteen minutes later, and by her expression, I could tell that something intense had happened in those fifteen minutes.

As we made our way in the Tercel over to the freeway, we tried to relay verbatim what the psychic had told each of us, but it was as if the words had already left us both. "Good thing we have the recording because I feel like my explanation of the reading isn't doing it any justice," Miette said after trying to convey what she had been told about her future. The gist of her reading was that things were going to get worse, then horrible, and then slowly get better, but in the end, if she made the choice to do so, she would end up happily married and would raise children with Sol.

"Maybe we should make a pact to listen to the recordings together. In exactly a year from today, we will play the recordings together and compare what was predicted with where we are then," I suggested, and Miette nodded. Suddenly, there was a crack of thunder, and I looked up to see that the sky had clouded over with a thick, dark rush of clouds. Just as we were driving up the on-ramp to the freeway, gigantic drops of water began falling from the sky and splattering across the windshield. The thunder continued to crack and roll all around us. As we drove farther out of the city, I turned around and looked back.

"Look, you can see where the line of clouds stops, and the sky turns blue and sunny right where the city ends," I observed, and I watched as a few lightning bolts flashed from the sky behind us while we continued driving out of New Orleans and into a beautiful, clear summer's day.

It was around noon, and we hadn't even begun to discuss where the day's drive would take us. As we drew closer to the East Coast, I began to wonder if we were getting closer to the end. But the end of what? Miette had a final destination, albeit an ambiguous one, since she had no idea what her life would look like when she arrived, but she had a destination and a person waiting for her. I had neither.

When I had left my parents' house, I hadn't known what to say. It was a slightly awkward goodbye because we didn't know what class of goodbye it was supposed to be, and my family had always leaned toward a more emotionally conservative com-munication style. One might even use the word "detached." I didn't know when I'd see them again: if it'd be a month, two months, or a year from then. Perhaps when the trip was over, which would be when I decided it was over, I would fly home and pick up my routine where I had left off. Or perhaps I'd stay on the East Coast and look for another service-industry routine, similar to the one I was escaping from. Nobody knew, which resulted in a very nonchalant "see you later" and a brief exchanging of hugs at the front door of our house.

I had my backpack, and I had some money in the bank. I had a few boxes of things stashed at my parents' house back home, but everything essential for my basic survival was in the car with me. I was a rolling stone, a wayfaring sailor, a vaga-bond with her roots ripped right out of the ground. A twenty-three-year-old woman on the road with nowhere to be and nobody waiting for her. What was I doing? What was the point of this whole thing? If I went back home after reaching Boston and fell into the same routine that was sending me down a road toward apathy and alcoholism, wouldn't it all have been in vain? I wanted to see what was out there, and I didn't think that by the time I reached Boston I would have done it.

Then I broke the silence that had been building in the car over the last forty minutes.

"What if I went back to Spain?"

Miette looked over at me, snapping herself out of her own deep thoughts and trying to get in sync with mine.

"Oh! Okay. That's an interesting idea..." she said, as if it were something we were going to discuss and decide together. As if my future were both of our responsibilities, and, in fact, it was. After weeks of consulting each other about every decision—what snacks to restock in the cooler, where to sleep, and even when and where to pee—it was natural that such an important life decision would be made between the two of us.

"Yeah. I mean, why not? You're going to New Jersey, and I have literally nothing on the East Coast. I was in Boston once looking at a photography school, but other than that, it's a foreign land to me."

"So do you mean to travel around Spain? Or look for a job there?"

"I don't think I can work there. All that red-tape bureaucracy crap." I pulled open my phone to look at the maximum amount of time I could be in Europe on a tourist visa. "I can stay for three months. So I could get a ticket there and get the return ticket for three months later."

"Yeah! Alright. This sounds like it has potential. So when and where would you fly from?"

I thought for a moment. It needed to be a place that was easy for us to get to in terms of our route to New Jersey and a place that I would want to return to after stomping around Spain for three months. "Well, what about Boston? It's just a little north of Jersey. I like the city. I've been there, and then I could think about if I want to go to that photography school in the end." It seemed logical enough. Miette agreed. I needed her approval to make sure that my impulses had at least some sense behind them, which just left us with the question of when I would go. I spent some time on various travel apps until I found a deal for a round trip to Sevilla at a fraction of the cost of all the other flights to Spain on all other dates that I tried. The only catch was that it left on July seventeenth. It was July fourteenth.

Miette nodded her head quickly and repeatedly to herself, looking out ahead at the road; it was her way of arbitrating her feelings about us being separated indefinitely in just three days' time. Finally, after she had mentally sorted it all out, she said with confidence and conviction, "Let's start the great race to Boston."

I punched in my information and hit "purchase tickets." I was going to Spain.

Georgia

THERE WAS THIS NEW HUMMING excitement in the car. Suddenly, after two weeks of going wherever the wind blew us, I had a direction. I had been secretly worried that when Miette got to New Jersey, I would have to face "reality" and re-integrate myself back into the churning wheel of society, falling back into the same routine of clocking in and clocking out of work, hitting last call and feeling listless. But now I had a plan! I would go to Spain. I would book a hostel for my first night in Sevilla and, from there, follow the yellow brick road.

Perusing the snack aisles in Harvey's Supermarket somewhere in the south of Georgia, we chatted about our more immediate plan. We had been rationing out grapes, string cheese, pita chips, and deli meat from our cooler, and we had developed a system where we would set a time to have a specific snack or drink in order to give us small joys to look forward to during our long, monotonous days in the car. I noticed that the snacks in the Georgia supermarket were different than the crunchy, hippie, granola snacks in our West Coast co-ops. We didn't find any whole wheat pita chips or rice cakes or trail mix, but we did find Spicy Cajun Crawtators Kettle Style Potato Chips and RV Cola to wash them down.

I listened to the conversations around me and noticed a thick, drowsy, and almost consonant-free English. This was the farthest from home I had ever felt within my own country. I felt like an authentic tourist, and I knew for certain that any of the people in the supermarket in that rural Georgian town, upon taking one glance at me, would think the same.

I had been talking to Shane sporadically over the previous few days. Nothing of great consequence, but I was trying to keep that little spark alive just in case. It was typical of me to fixate on a certain person, especially after sex. A few hours earlier, we had been talking about whether we'd ever see each other again when I stealthily prompted him to propose the idea that we direct our route toward Atlanta, Georgia and pay him a visit. Examining a box of Moon Pie marshmallow cookies, I asked Miette what she thought about sleeping in Atlanta. It was on the way to Boston, and now that we had a place to be in three days, it fit our trajectory perfectly. She thought it was a great idea, and I think we were both eager for a little bit of boy drama to give us a fresh topic of conversation for the road.

Back in the car, I entertained myself by looking for cheap hotels. I figured that after our many nights in seedy hostels and our various car-sleeps, we could treat ourselves to one night in a four-star hotel. The thought of seeing Shane again sent a mostly pleasant anxiety tingling over my body, and I felt a nervous clenching in my gut. Would it be as natural the second time?

The hours passed along with the miles. We were now driving north for the first time in weeks, and everything was different. Tired and a little cranky, we were finally arriving at the city. The freeway was immense. There were more lanes than I had ever seen on one road, with additional lanes splitting off and looping around above and below us, with overpasses and underpasses everywhere I looked. It was clearly rush hour, and on top of that, it was getting dark. Poor Miette, flustered and overwhelmed, cursed at the car that had just cut her off, at the car honking because she had cut him off, and at the city of Atlanta for building such an impossible freeway. When we finally found our exit, we were three lanes away and screamed as we watched it fly by. It was mayhem and we were at our hangriest—when hunger leads to anger—and by the time we made it into the city and figured out how to get to the hotel, both of us were on the edge of tears.

Checking in to the hotel, I felt posh and important and yet somehow out of place. I felt like a fraud—feeling posh and important wasn't what our trip was about. But then again, what was our trip about? There were no rules. In fact, the trip could be about there being no rules.

I scanned the card and opened the door to a beautiful, clean hotel room. I dropped my backpack on the floor and flung myself onto the bed. I was engulfed in the comforter, and the smell of clean laundry fluffed into the air. From the bathroom, I heard Miette marvel at the bathtub and the fluffy white towels folded neatly on the edge.

"Shoot. I think I'll just stay here tonight. Screw Shane!" My words were muffled by the comforter because I was still sprawled face down on the bed. When Miette asked what I was going to wear, I laughed. I really didn't consider her or myself to be the kind of girl that meticulously picked out her outfit when going to meet a boy, but in reality, I think we're all sometimes that kind of girl. And then the gravity of the question sank in. *What am I going to wear?* After a revitalizing shower, the following hour was a frenzied session of dress-up. We tried every combination of my seven articles of clothing until I settled on a pair of denim shorts and the same off-the-shoulder, gray-and-white, tie-dyed top that I had been wearing all week. To be fair, my options were slim.

Miette dropped me off at the bar where Shane was waiting after assuring me that she would be fine with whatever I decided to do later. She was very much looking forward to a long bath and some quality phone time with her husband. I got out of the car somewhat awkwardly, noticing that my coordination was off and my anxiety levels were off the charts. I could usually count on my social grace to be able to command any room, except when that critical, little, self-doubt gremlin would sneak up onto my shoulder and whisper all of my flaws into my ear. I took a deep breath and flicked him off my shoulder, reassuring myself that I wasn't a desperate floozy and that Shane didn't think that either. Atlanta had been directly on our path to Boston and was also coincidentally where he lived. It's not like I had driven seven hours from New Orleans just to see him.

He was standing by the entrance to the bar. As I got closer, he looked up, and a smile flashed across his face. *That smile.* He casually pulled my chair out for me when we reached the table on the patio. We ordered two whiskey gingers and started chatting like old friends, although I don't normally play with my hair as much or nervously apply ChapStick with my old friends.

"So what's new in the last couple days?" he asked, chewing on a piece of ice from his drink.

"God, it seems like so much has happened. We camped at the Grand Canyon—"

"Nice! I miss that place."

"Yeah. Well, in reality, we didn't camp. We got stoned and slept in the car on the edge of a cliff," I admitted. He laughed.

"Okay. Then what?"

"I'm pretty sure we saw the devil in New Orleans," I said.

"You *what?*"

"Yeah, it was one of those moments where we both knew something really weird had happened without even talking to each other about it. We were walking down this really creepy street. Dudes dressed in all black would walk by, and I just imagined them opening their trench coats up and having dead rats and skulls hanging off of the inside lining. But anyways, there was this group of people huddled up in a corner, and this one guy with a black hood on looked at us really fast, made this piercing eye contact, and then looked away. But wait—the thing is that his eyes were entirely black."

"What the..." he said with his eyebrows raised. "Sounds like a bad acid trip."

As the conversation progressed, we compared fantasy books to fantasy films and discussed his aspirations of becoming a pediatrician. After we had finished our very stiff drinks, I asked him what he felt like doing.

"I feel like having a lot of sex." My muscles tensed instantly upon hearing his response. Obviously, that's what we were doing, that's what I had redirected my route to Atlanta for, but hearing it said so blatantly made me feel uneasy and exposed. I wanted to at least pretend that there was more substance to our meeting.

I rolled my eyes and a micro-expression of confusion dashed across his face. He was obviously not concerned with formalities nor with what this all looked like, and why should he be? Yet again, I felt an almost unidentifiable guilt creep over me with a little splash of self-loathing and embarrassment. The fact that we were both consenting adults, we were both attracted to each other, and that we had already spent some time getting to know each other wasn't enough to allow the feminist part of my brain to convince the brainwashed-by-society part that there was nothing innately slutty about a casual hookup.

We got into his car and headed over to his apartment. I was a little tipsy from the double whiskey and wasn't paying much attention to my surroundings, but I did notice a wooden cross on the wall by his bed and a lot of white: white walls, white blanket, white, white, and white. Luckily my anxiety about our time together being more awkward the second time was unfounded, despite our having consumed significantly less alcohol than the night we met.

After everyone was satisfied, we lay in blissful silence. Then, just minutes later, Shane asked me where I wanted him to drop me off. Again, my muscles tensed, and I felt my face get hot. He was kicking me out! I felt like I was in one of those typical embarrassing scenes in a chick flick, where the main character is a sympathetic Kristen Wiig type who doesn't ever seem to catch the hint. If we were strictly here for sex and we couldn't even have a second drink at the bar, why would I have expected to stay the night? I was not used to one-night stands, or two-night stands, or any other version of sex with a man that I wasn't in an exclusive relationship with.

"You actually want to put on all your clothes and drive me all the way to the hotel right now? At midnight?" I asked, already knowing the answer. I was so comfortable, and my arms and legs were weights, pressing into the mattress. At this point, I didn't even care about the emotional implications. I was so exhausted that the thought of getting up and putting all of the pieces of my outfit and my life back together, which had been thrown carelessly around the room, made me groan.

"No, I don't want to at all. I want to stay here and enjoy the sex-coma I'm about to fall into, but I have to leave for the hospital at 5:30 a.m. I have an early shift."

"Well, why don't you just drop me off in the morning?" It made sense to me. Why get dressed twice when he had the option of only getting dressed once? It didn't even occur to me that he may actually just want to be alone. It didn't occur to me because I had never slept with someone whose presence felt like a burden.

"You really want to wake up at 5 a.m.? If you're cool with that, I'm cool with that. I just assumed you would rather sleep in tomorrow."

The next morning, before the crack of dawn, Shane gave me a lift to the hotel. When I stepped out of the car, he surprised me by also stepping out and by giving me a long, passionate kiss in the parking lot. I didn't have the energy to analyze what it all meant. I needed to drag Miette down to the breakfast buffet for coffee and pancakes, and I wanted to smoke a cigarette. When I got to the room, she was curled up in a compact little ball in the center of the king-size bed, lost in a sea of blankets and pillows.

I dropped my purse onto the floor and then allowed myself to collapse down next to it. With my elbows on my knees and my head in my hands, I let out a huge sigh and sunk into my inner world of insecurity. I felt like a complete idiot, and yet at the same time, I was giddy with the excitement of Shane's kiss.

I felt my eyes moisten, and when I scrunched them closed, a tear spilled onto the floor. What I was so upset about wasn't precisely clear, but the feelings of shame and embarrassment were definitely there. I went to the bathroom to clean myself up, and I heard Miette stirring in the mass of blankets.

"Good morning, sunshine!" I called, trying to cover up my distress, but I was sure my shaky voice would give it away. "How did you sleep?"

She sat up clumsily. With her glorious bedhead and her eyes squinting at the daylight, she reminded me of a sleepy meerkat popping its head out of the hole before it had completely woken up. A smile spread across my face, and the world was right again. Who gave a shit if a dumb boy wanted me to stay over or not? I had the best friend in the world who I knew would always want me to stay. I had never doubted that Miette knew me to the core and loved me just as deeply, which should have been ten times more valuable to my sense of self-worth than anything a guy I had met the week before said or did. And yet the mere existence of sexual attraction had let something external and altogether trivial, such as a hookup, mess with my self-perception. I wasn't a slut. I wasn't desperate. I wanted something and I went and got it, and I didn't get up and get dressed in the middle of the night because I didn't fucking feel like it. I went to sleep, and now I was with my best friend, ready to enjoy the last days of our epic adventure. Everything was good.

We ate our breakfast and were back in the Tercel, which had become the closest thing to home that we had had over the past two weeks. Remembering the stress we experienced getting into Atlanta, we were both fraught with anxiety about getting back on the seven-lane freeway. Before that could even happen, we first had to find it. We were clumsy navigating our way through the overwhelming 6 a.m. traffic. After missing our turn several times and having circled the block repeatedly, my GPS directed us to turn onto a road with a giant "Construction Zone" sign blocking the street. I could see the parallel street that we needed to reach, and the construction zone was an unnecessary and unappreciated obstacle.

"What do I do?" Miette shrieked in frustration. She was the driver, and I was the navigator. We had accepted our roles, and I knew that whatever I said to do would be done without question. I was fed up, and my impulses got the best of me.

"Turn. Just turn! Fuck them. I want to get out of this place!" She swerved the car up onto the sidewalk, barely dodging the construction sign. We were off roading in our '96 Tercel. We screamed in unison as we avoided gaping pits in the asphalt and piles of cement until we made our way out of the danger zone and incorporated ourselves into normal traffic. Miette looked at me with an expression of fear and satisfaction, trying to decide whether to scold me or laugh. Naturally, we ended up laughing.

Maryland

O N THE FREEWAY, ONCE WE had left the chaos of the city and the hordes of frantic people rushing to work behind us, we were free to organize our last three days. At the moment, all we had to do was pick a target between Atlanta and Boston and shoot for it. We decided to just drive north until we almost couldn't stand driving anymore and then check the map to see if there were any interesting towns nearby. The wet marshlands transformed into rolling green fields as we drove through the Carolinas, and by the time we were in Virginia, it was too dark to appreciate the landscape.

After nearly ten hours of driving we were both feeling delirious, and it was time to settle on our destination. I was anything but familiar with the East Coast. It was a mysterious land, but the name "Ocean City, Maryland" suddenly came to my mind.

One hung-over summer's day, I had been watching daytime television with a friend, and a program came on about Ocean City. Watching the pasty, visored Americans stroll down the beach and dab their toes in the cool Atlantic waters, we joked about vacationing there instead of his usual trip to Belize. Since nothing else sounded familiar, Miette and I decided to suffer through two more hours of driving and get to Ocean City. I smiled as we made our decision, thinking of my friend and what he would say if he knew where I was heading. He would probably ask me to buy him a hat.

Entering Ocean City, we saw one cop car after another, and although we weren't doing anything illegal, I always had trouble getting along with police officers. Upon seeing the distant glow of those red and blue lights, adrenaline shot through my veins. Were they hunting an escaped convict? Were they looking for drunk drivers? Or was there just that much crime in Ocean City? So much that each block was assigned its own patrol car? I didn't feel the happy-go-lucky-let's-go-fly-kites vibes. I felt paranoid.

We drove around the town with the windows down, our backs sticky with sweat from the humidity, considering our sleeping options. We had already made the decision to do a car-sleep that night, but the question was where we were going to park the car. We found a small parking lot on a residential block, and as soon as Miette had turned off the ignition, I popped open two beers that I had grabbed from the cooler. Each sip was a beautiful relief from the muggy eighty-five degrees that actually felt like one hundred. We drank our beers and then opened another two. After those were finished, we had to pee—our bodies had synchronized so perfectly that our basic needs were even coordinated—so we took turns sliding out of the car and hiding between a trash bin and the brick wall to squat, keeping our eyes out for patrol cars.

"Miette, I cannot sleep like this," I said in frustration. We had rolled the windows up in the car, leaving just a crack of ventilation, but the humidity was too suffocating. The windows were opaque with the steam from our breath, and I could feel drops of sweat form on parts of my body that I didn't even know had sweat glands.

"Yeah, this isn't going to work," she replied, also admitting defeat.

In front of us was a beautiful green lawn with lush, well-trimmed grass. On the lawn was also a house, somebody's private property, but the grass looked so comfortable in comparison to the stiff car seats. Sleeping outdoors seemed much more logical than suffocating to death in the closed and locked car. I grabbed a towel and threw it down on the lawn, near the car. Miette, seeing my expression of relief, followed right behind me.

It was around two a.m. when we had lay down on the grass, and when the sun began creeping up over the ocean, I opened my eyes to the light of dawn. The air was fresh, much more so than the night before. I looked at my phone; it was just after six a.m. I closed my eyes and drifted back to sleep.

"Excuse me. Hey, excuse me!" I was jolted awake by a deep, nearby voice, and upon opening my eyes, I saw an older, bearded man standing over us. He was nicely dressed, but he did not have a nice expression on his face. "You can't sleep here. The service is about to start, and I'm sorry, but I can't have you sleeping on beach towels on the church lawn."

I looked up at the house in front of me, and I could see clearly in the daylight that it was a church. How we hadn't noticed the steeple and the cross the night before baffled me, but there they were, in all their glory. The man started walking toward the door, and I scrambled up and reached over to shake Miette awake.

"Hey, dude. The pastor guy is here. He seems pissed."

"The pastor what?" She rubbed her eyes and blinked at me. She clearly understood as much of what I had said as if I had been speaking to her in Mandarin.

"We're sleeping on a church lawn."

We grabbed our towels and got into the car, and as we drove past the church, I waved at the pastor, shouting, "Have a wonderful service!" I didn't know if I were being ironic or sincere, but I was definitely emphatic. It was still early, and the streets of Ocean City were empty so we drove toward the beach.

The Atlantic Ocean was bluer and fresher looking than the mysterious, dark green Pacific Ocean that I had grown up with. We sat in the silky sand and sipped our coffees in the morning light, as we rested under the weight of everything we had lived recently. The air tossed my hair around my face, and I thought about how perfect the wind was in that moment. I felt like I was blowing in the wind, that the pieces of my life were up in the air and could land anywhere at any point. This was the feeling of adventure at its purest, but it also felt like the deep breath you take when you know something is coming to an end.

In two days, I would be boarding an airplane and flying to another continent, where I knew no one and barely spoke the language. I would be leaving my best friend behind. We had become so unified over the month we had spent together. I looked down at my tattoo, the arrow flying across my tanned skin, and smiled. I glanced over at Miette's bicep. *Two arrows from the same quiver.*

The white noise of the wind took away any feeling of obligation to talk, and we sat in blissful, contemplative silence, both gazing far out into the ocean as well as deep into ourselves. It felt so perfect not knowing what was going to happen. I felt like I was turning myself over to destiny, truly giving the Universe the opportunity to show me what I needed to see and take me to what I needed to experience. *I'm all yours, Universe!* I thought. *I'm ready for all of it!*

We brought our laundry up to a laundromat and wandered back down to the beach to have something to eat. The sun was making its way up the sky, and people were now flocking to the seafront promenade. We sat down at the bar in a little café, which was decorated with surfboards and other beach-life paraphernalia. The bartender was a tattooed woman in her late thirties, whose skin had been made tough by the sand and the sea. Her hair and her eyes were dark but had a warm, sun-kissed glow. She asked us for our stories as she served us our brunch tacos and Bloody Marys. We gave her a brief version of what we were up to so far from home, and she smiled nostalgically.

"I was there once, traveling around, not knowing where I was supposed to be. I'm from the Midwest, and when I came here to Ocean City, I fell in love." While she said those words, I wondered if something similar would happen to me. Would I find myself somewhere and just know that it was where I was meant to be? At that moment, I only knew that I didn't know anything.

We finished our food and took a walk down the promenade, dazzled by the incredible sand creations and a sky full of kites. Most of the sculptures people had made were dedicated to Jesus and were incredibly intricate. I wondered how early these people had woken up in order to finish their masterpieces before noon. After an invigorating walk along the beach and a quick swim in the Atlantic Ocean, we collected our laundry and began our drive to Newport, Rhode Island, which was the destination we had arbitrarily chosen that morning. It would be about a seven-hour drive, getting us there with plenty of time to check in to the motel we had booked and leisurely enjoy our last evening together.

New York

RIVING NORTH ON A LONG stretch of freeway during one of our quieter periods in the car, we saw the sign for New Jersey. As if it were normal to erupt into choreographed song and dance and as if it had been planned ahead, both of us, at exactly the same moment, sang at the top of our lungs, "The final countdown!"

I looked over at Miette, and she looked back at me, the two of us horrified at the coincidence that had just occurred. We sat in awkward silence for a few seconds, processing.

"What *was* that?" she asked, aghast.

"The weirdest thing that has ever happened to me in the history of my life, that's what," I responded, equally as shaken. Had our brains merged into one? Had we developed telepathy?

We drove through New Jersey, and Miette sent a playful message to her husband, who was currently in the same state, eagerly awaiting her arrival. Unfortunately, he didn't respond as playfully, taking offense at our driving through New Jersey without stopping to see him. What he didn't understand was that we were in a different mentality than the rest of the world. The road trip had become a lifestyle, and we were not ready to leave the dream and touch down to the reality of Miette's relationship crisis. Not until I got on that plane in Boston.

We continued on our route to Newport, and as I was studying the map on my phone, I had a realization. We were about to drive past New York City! I had never been to New York, and although we wouldn't be entering Manhattan, the idea of seeing the New York skyline was exhilarating. As the buildings took form across the Hudson River, Lana del Rey's sultry voice came over the car speakers during her song "Diet Mountain Dew." The city was glorious, even from a distance. Suddenly we were confronted by another maze of overpasses and lanes merging together just like in Atlanta, and we quickly lost our way. After a whirlwind of cars, lanes, honking, merging, screaming and frantically trying to update the GPS, we found ourselves stuck in the middle of the Bronx in rush hour traffic.

Miette pulled the car over onto the side of the road so that we could catch our breath after the hectic fifteen minutes that had just flown by. In reality, it wasn't to catch our breath but rather to prevent a mental breakdown. We were still hours and a few states away from Newport, which seemed insignificant compared to the monstrous task of finding our way out of New York's northernmost borough. With this information in mind, we were feeling vulnerable parked on that backstreet next to graffitied walls that towered over piles of garbage and broken glass.

While we were sitting in the parked car getting our bearings, Miette's phone started going off. She swiped it open to look at her messages and immediately the air in the car changed. Sol was so upset that we had driven through New Jersey without stopping to see him that he told her not to bother going to New Jersey even when the trip was over. That message was an alarm going off in the middle of a beautiful dream. She was devastated and trembling. Would that be the end of her marriage? Because of one small failure to meet his expectations, was her husband, who had been drunk and putting her down for weeks, telling her he never wanted to see her again? Was that even possible?

She cried with her head against the steering wheel, and I rubbed her back, desperate for a way to console her. "Whatever happens, you are so strong, and nothing is too big for you. If you guys have to break up, there will be life, *beautiful life*, afterward." I winced upon pronouncing the words "break up" because I was recognizing for the first time that this was a possibility. "There is always a way. You just have to take it step by step, moment by moment, and make the right decisions for *you*." I felt like I was repeating those inspirational phrases that you find scrolling through social media, and although they were trite and cliché, I believed them. More than desiring to convince her that that everything would work out and she and her husband would find a way to resolve their issues, I wanted to reassure her that she would be okay and empower her to find her happiness, with or without him. I wanted to free her of the feelings of guilt and fear that could potentially color her decisions about how to move forward.

She stopped her heaving and sat for a moment, her muscles limp and her eyes swollen, exhausted from the intense storm of emotion that had just hijacked her body. "Where do I go?" she asked meekly, beginning to understand that apart from her husband in New Jersey, she had nowhere and nobody outside of Bellingham, which was thousands of miles away.

"Miette, I didn't want to pressure you before. And I know that the idea of talking to your mom about all of this makes you die a little bit inside, but I think it's time you called her and told her about everything that's going on between you and Sol." She sighed deeply and nodded. "You have nothing to be ashamed of. If I were a mom and my daughter was going through something like this and she didn't tell me, I would be devastated that she didn't trust me enough to confide in me."

Rhode Island

E PULLED OURSELVES TOGETHER JUST enough to make it out of the Bronx and complete our three-hour commute to Newport. The hotel we had booked was small and in the middle of a field. The lobby looked more like a kitchen from the fifties with an old television on the wall and a bowl of shiny apples on a small table, which was decorated with a doily tablecloth. The woman who checked us in had a long, gray ponytail and an austere, ankle-length dress. When we arrived at our room, Miette began to cry again. I pulled out my little box of tricks and insisted that she swallowed a valium and take a hot shower. While I listened to her in the shower sobbing, I imagined her sitting on the floor, the water steaming the room and dripping down her face with her tears. It was beyond heartbreaking.

I took a walk and left her to her conversation with her mom. When I returned, she told me that her mom had been incredibly supportive, that she had told her about a distant cousin in Massachusetts, that she would find her contact information, and ask if Miette could stay with her for a while until she could think clearly about what to do next. It was a perfect short-term solution to a potentially long-term and hideous problem. To help her sleep, I gave her another valium, and we both slept through the night.

The next morning, her face had a healthy glow. I've always been a believer in getting to sleep as quickly as possible when suffering any type of emotional distress because everything seems more manageable in the morning. It reminded me that no matter how bad we feel, we always wake up with a chance to do things differently. As we got ready to leave, I realized that this would be the last time I would pack my backpack in the United States because in less than twenty-four hours, I would be in Sevilla. I went outside to locate all of my possessions that had found new homes in various corners of the Tercel and started to divide them into two piles: "Bring to Spain" and "Leave with Miette."

"Ugh," I said, as I pulled out my sweatshirt. "Pismo. Keep or leave?" I held it up and realized that despite the horrible day that it represented, I had almost become fond of it, and I shoved it into my backpack. We loaded our things and ourselves into the car and drove through the historic town of Newport, Rhode Island. It had a clean, New England, seafaring atmosphere. We ambled unhurriedly along the docks in the sunshine and had lunch in a Thai restaurant, which for us, after three weeks of mainly turkey sandwiches and cooler snacks, was a luxurious feast. When we got back into the car, I put Boston Logan International Airport into the GPS.

As I typed in the words, I almost couldn't believe where we were going. In two hours, I would be in the airport, about to embark on a solo journey to Europe. We spent the two hours talking nonstop, as if we had to cram in every important conversation to hold us over during my long journey until I could call her from Spain. We talked about everything, and before I knew it, we were entering the city, and above the freeway was an exit sign for Logan International.

Massachusetts

IETTE PULLED UP TO THE airport and stopped the car. That was it. We were at a crossroads. So much had happened over the last three weeks. All of the places we had seen and the people we had met flashed through my mind like an old VHS tape on fast forward, and I felt like a changed person. I also felt a deeper understanding of our friendship; those three weeks would shape our relationship and be the glue that held us together for the rest of our lives, no matter where either of us ended up. And now, after overcoming nearly twenty years of obstacles together, we were being let loose to face our battles alone. Was I ready?

She scrambled awkwardly out of the car and scurried over to give me a hug as I tugged my backpack out of the trunk and onto the sidewalk.

"I love you, Dunes," she said, her head nestled in my shoulder.

"I love you to tiny little pieces, Swamps."

We both released each other from the hug and whipped around quickly, knowing that otherwise we'd end up in tears. I grabbed my pack and grunted as I pulled it on over my shoulders. As she drove away, a strange sensation came over me—an unlikely combination of panic and acceptance. I walked up the stairs, into the airport, and to the check-in line. After passing through security, I wandered around the airport in a daze. I realized I wanted a snack, and for the first time in weeks, I bought myself food without consulting my best friend to see if she were also hungry.

I fanned myself with my boarding pass while I waited to get on the plane. My row of seats was empty, so I lifted up the armrests and stretched out my legs. The airplane took off into the late afternoon sky. I ordered a glass of red wine and popped a valium, and six hours later, I awoke well-rested and ready to make my connecting flight in Madrid. I had traveled overseas three times before so I had been previously prepared for the agony of long-haul flights, but that had been by far the easiest and most comfortable flight I had ever taken. During the entire hour-long journey from Madrid to Sevilla,I let my head rest against the wall as I gazed out the window, as if the horizon were a crystal ball and in the clouds were painted images of the future. I watched them swirl into shapes of what could be, and I realized that not knowing what would happen didn't give me anxiety. In fact, I had found comfort in accepting that I could neither predict nor prepare for most of what was painted in those clouds. In relinquishing control, I was rewarded with a sense of inner peace. Hypnotized by the horizon, I was in a state of serenity, and the butterflies that I had felt leaving Washington were now resting calmly in my stomach.

Sevilla

I got off the plane, collected my backpack, and stepped outside into the dry Spanish heat. It was mid-morning, but the sun was already cooking the asphalt, and the small airport was nearly empty. I was the only person outside. In my daydreamy state, I hadn't done any travel preparation, apart from booking one night in a hostel, whose address I hadn't even written down. I had truly handed myself over to fate.

A bus pulled up, and I got on, without asking where it would take me. As we drove into town, I marveled at the buildings, the people, and the horse-drawn carriages. When I saw a river, which usually passes through the cultural epicenter of a city, I had the feeling that we were entering the historic center of Sevilla, and I got off the bus. It was like the entire previous month had been preparing me for this moment. I wasn't scared or apprehensive. I was ready.

My mind was flooded with flashbacks of my summer in Salamanca four years prior. I had spent most of my previous time in Spain in Castilla y León, which is one of the country's seventeen autonomous communities and lies to the Northeast of Madrid. It is also home to the University city of Salamanca, where people hiss the "s" in Spanish words and are generally friendly, polite, and mild-mannered. During that summer abroad, I formed my first impression of Spain, and I didn't realize that the amount of cultural diversity that could be discovered in a country smaller than Texas would compete with what I had recently seen crossing the entire United States.

Hunched over with my backpack strapped to my shoulders, I smacked my sandals on the ground with each deliberate step, careful not to slip under the weight of all of my possessions. I pulled my phone out of my pocket to look at the time—because that's all I could use it for now that I was in another country—and I knew that I wouldn't be able to do anything until I found Wi-fi. I was in no hurry to solve my Wi-fi dilemma, and figured I would amble about for while and see if it would solve itself. Just then, I looked up and saw a Starbucks right across the street from me. Although Starbucks was born in Seattle, I had always seen it as just another money-hungry, multinational corporation and would usually opt for small, locally-owned coffee shops that had open mic nights, monthly art exhibitions, and tattooed baristas. However, this time when I saw the green-and-white two-tailed mermaid, I felt grounded, like a little piece of home was there with me, watching over me and offering me Wi-Fi. I crossed the street and dumped my pack onto the sidewalk next to one of the tables and arched my back with my hands on my hips to work out all of the kinks that had accumulated during my travels.

"*Disculpa, podría vigilarme la mochila por favor?*" I asked a woman sitting at the table next to mine. I was nervous, and the Spanish words felt awkward coming out of my mouth, as if my lips and tongue were taken by surprise upon being asked to make those foreign shapes and sounds.

"I'm sorry. What?" she responded, which I should have expected because Starbucks is where the tourists would conglomerate, most of them experiencing a similar sensation of safety when in a foreign country, even if they weren't from Seattle.

"Oh, sorry! Would you mind watching my pack for just a moment while I go inside? I would just take it, but as you can see, it's a bit of a beast, and it's pretty crowded in there," I said and laughed.

"Of course. Don't worry, dear. I'll make sure it's safe," she replied in her melodic English accent.

I came back out of the Starbucks with a giant iced Americano, the Wi-Fi password, and a big smile on my face. I pulled out my phone and found my reservation for the hostel. As I studied the map, I couldn't believe my luck; the hostel was just around the corner. Of all the possible places in the capital city of Andalusia, I had gotten off the random bus at a random stop a block away from my hostel, whose name I didn't even know at the time.

I hoisted up my pack and, iced coffee in hand, triumphantly flip-flopped my way down the winding alley in search of my new temporary home. Most Spanish people wouldn't be caught dead wearing flip-flops in public, and it's an incredibly rare sight to see a Spaniard, at least those born in the twentieth century, walking as they drink or eat. Those two details, plus my gigantic backpack and fair complexion, screamed, "I am not from here!"

I arrived at the hostel and checked in. I was surrounded by languages, American English being the least common of them all. I was impressed at how fluidly the receptionist, a tattooed twenty-something with severe bedhead, switched from one language to another. The atmosphere was hectic. Several travelers darted around the room and up and down the stairs; a few Germans were on the couches, opening their backpacks and rummaging through their possessions; some Spaniards were laughing loudly in the kitchen, waving around their cans of Cruzcampo beer; and a few Chinese girls sat in the stairwell Skyping loudly with their friends in Mandarin.

I lumbered up the stairs to the third flour, which was actually the fourth floor, because in Spain, the first floor is called the ground floor instead of the first floor like in the States, which caused me some confusion. I arrived dripping with sweat and out of breath, but I was relieved to find that the room was empty, and I could settle into my bunk bed calmly and without the awkwardness of being in a small room together with strangers because I was not in the mood for small talk. I took a shower, scrubbing off all of the sweat and travel grease and emerged from the bathroom feeling like a new woman. I lay down on my bed, turned the fan directly toward me, and let out a deep sigh. I was alone in a foreign country with no agenda.

After a few minutes, I flipped over and pulled out my laptop, suddenly overcome with the urge to look at my photos from the road trip with a premature feeling of nostalgia. How was Miette? Had she found her long-lost relative's house? Had she spoken to Sol? I sent her a message informing her that I had arrived safely at Sevilla and to call me as soon as she woke up.

As I rearranged my photos, I heard some commotion in the hall, and two tall, bohemian, northern-European-looking guys walked into the room, laughing loudly and speaking what I assumed was either German or Dutch. They were both wearing smiles from ear to ear and brought with them a contagious enthusiasm, but even so, I wasn't sure if I were ready to socialize. One of them asked me what I was working on, and I explained the photo essay I was putting together about my trip. Rene—the thinner, freckled one with high cheekbones and seductive, ice-blue eyes—took off his straw fedora and leaned over to look at my pictures.

"That's amazing. You just traveled across the United States and now here you are in Sevilla," he said in perfect American English. The other guy's name was Peter. He was beefier and had on a tank top and a leather necklace, and he spoke with a deep, booming voice, with which he asked me how long I had been in Spain. His eyes were sweet, and he reminded me of a big brown bear. Despite his voice and his size, he seemed timid.

"A couple of hours," I responded.

"What? That's it? You literally just got here!" exclaimed Rene. He was the more gregarious and confident of the two, perhaps a lover of attention and quite possibly a Don Juán. We talked for a while, and then they headed up to the roof to check out the pool and bar, where I said I'd meet them in a while.

An hour later, I opened the door to a rooftop paradise. There was a small pool from which you could see rooftops with rust-colored, ceramic shingles. Next to the pool was a bar and a row of wooden tables. Rene and Peter were in the pool chatting with some fellow travelers. I let my dress drop to the ground, and I slipped into the chilly water.

"So, Kate. Where are you from?" asked Rene.

"Seattle," I said because it was more efficient than explaining that I was from a town called Bellingham that was an hour and a half to the north of Seattle. For a split second, I considered making up a whole new identity just for kicks, as I had frequently done with my friend, Marguerite, when we were traveling around Southern France and Spain. I loved to speak with fake accents in bars and pretend to be her Eastern European friend.

"Ahh, no way!" gushed Peter. "Pearl Jam is my favorite band. You guys made grunge. That's so awesome!" They explained that they were from different parts of the Netherlands, and suddenly feeling more sociable, I told them about my Dutch lineage. They were impressed, although when I pronounced my last name for them, they couldn't control their laughter.

I spelled it out for them, and Rene said, "That's a really cool last name. It sounds like royalty. Do you know what it means?"

I shook my head.

"Yeah, that is a really good last name. It means, like, the keeper of the peace. But not when you pronounce it like that." Peter chuckled.

We spent the following fifteen minutes working on my pronunciation of my own name until I finally gave up. "Whatever you guys. I'm just going to pronounce it the really cool American way."

They told me they were going to a bullfight later and asked if I'd like to join them. I had no plans for that evening, or any other evening of my life for that matter, so I agreed to go. I had very little concept of what a bullfight was, and if I had, I would most definitely have declined, but I decided to roll with the punches.

We left the hostel and began our walk down the streets of Sevilla to the Plaza de Toros. The direct and scorching rays of the afternoon sun softened and lengthened as the hours passed, casting long shadows across the ground. Everyone's skin looked flawless and tanned in that golden evening light, and every building and balcony was suddenly photogenic.

As we walked, Rene told me about how his mom was from Sevilla and that's why he spoke Spanish like he did, with an Andalusian accent. I couldn't help feeling a little bit envious of this well-educated, broad-minded, polylingual, bohemian Dutchman. I had studied Spanish for years in university and didn't even feel competent enough to buy a pack of cigarettes in Spanish.

We stopped at a tapas bar before the show, and I had no idea what to do. The names of the food made no sense to me, and I didn't understand how to order. At that point, I still believed that tapas were a type of food and not a portion size. I ended up with a slice of egg and potato *tortilla* on a piece of mayonnaise-slathered baguette and an adorable little glass that appeared to contain no more than five sips of beer. We walked to the bullring, and I was suddenly overwhelmed by the mass of people pushing their way through the various doors leading into the dusty stadium. We took our seats, and the show began.

Three dainty, yet somehow macho, men in tights and short, sparkly jackets glided on horseback into the ring. The bull was released, and the crowd cheered. I remembered a book my mother used to read to me when I was a child called *Ferdinand the Friendly Bull*, who would talk to butterflies and look for shapes in the clouds. Suddenly it made sense to me why Ferdinand being friendly made him different from the "toro bravo" because this bull came pummeling out of his stall, kicking up dust and spewing steam from his nose.

To my horror, one of the matadors on horseback lunged a spear into the back of his neck. My body tensed, and I let out a small shriek. What was I thinking coming to a bullfight? I was thinking it would be a cultural experience when in reality it was glorified animal cruelty. The massacre continued, and the previously growling and invincible-looking beast, having now been stabbed and slashed and pierced, began to stumble and became dizzy in his attacks.

The matador, who wore the most sparkly and most ostentatious jacket of the three, held up the famous red cape and began taunting the bull, swerving out of the way at the last moment as the bull charged. With the spear in hand, he shoved it between the bull's shoulders in an attempt to pierce his aorta and deliver the fatal blow. Unfortunately, this particular matador was clumsy, and the bull continued to fight back through his suffering. Now with various spears wedged into his back and blood dripping all over him, the bull slowly lost his power.

As I watched the scene, tears streamed down my face. I felt a deep empathy for the bull and was overcome with a sudden desire to see him trample the matador, crushing his tiny skull with one fierce stamp of the hoof. How could this torture be considered entertainment? The people around me cheered and waved little white napkins in the air. I stood on the bench in order to see through the crowds, and suddenly felt unstable, like I was going to collapse to the ground. Finally, the bull went down, and I could hear a desperate wailing inside of my head. I felt the pain and terror of the bull as he gave in and accepted his defeat.

The matador stood tall and proud, took off his hat, and bowed before the roaring crowd. He was given a bouquet of flowers, and he sashayed victoriously around the ring as he haughtily accepted his praise. I looked over at Peter and Rene. My eyes were wet, and my cheeks smeared with mascara. "I need to leave. I don't feel good," I said as I began to push my way through the crowd, desperately searching for an escape from the horror of the bullfight. There were still five more bulls to go, but there was no way in hell I was staying one minute more. I thought of all the animals I had ever loved, and my heart was heavy with grief for the bull who had been slaughtered and the five more who were about to fight for their lives and lose.

I wasn't in the mood to talk about it. Once we were out of

the ring, I told the Dutch boys that I had experienced an attack of claustrophobia. They chatted about how they weren't too impressed with the experience and didn't mind leaving early, but they were in no way as affected as I was. We stopped for beers along the way back to wherever we were going, and by midnight, we were sitting on the sidewalk with plastic cups in our hands, surrounded by a mass of drunk, young people who were talking about life, philosophy, and where to score blow.

When I finally fell into my bunk bed, feeling my jetlag, sleep came over me effortlessly. I slept deeply and soundly until I was resurrected at three p.m. the next day. After splashing water on my face and getting my bearings, I wandered up to the rooftop to find Rene and Peter hanging around the pool.

"Vredevoogd!" they cheered with that perfect pronunciation of my last name that I would never achieve. They asked me if I wanted to join them to see the Alcázar. Having done no research, I had no idea what that was, but it sounded cultural and interesting. Maintaining my go-with-the-flow attitude, I agreed.

The Alcázar was one of Spain's most important monumental compounds from the Arabic period and was a visual delicacy for my Western eyes. We wandered through the gardens and palaces, which were intricately decorated with colorful, hand-painted tiles, and trickling fountains. There was a peaceful beauty enclosed within the walls of the compound, as well as a feeling of great history. I felt like I had discovered a small, hidden paradise. It was as if I had walked into the secret garden. I imagined dark-eyed women draped in silk dipping their fingertips in the pools of water and gliding them over the surface as they strolled down the corridors. I reached down to touch the water myself, and with the cool contact, I was transported back in time to the tenth century.

When we emerged from the Alcázar, we decided that the next appropriate cultural activity would be to visit the Plaza de España. It was a beautiful square surrounded by a small river. It had an impressive fountain in the center, reflecting rainbows in the mist. We relaxed in the shade of the sculptures before heading back to the hostel to make dinner. I noticed myself feeling like I was part of a group, like the three of us were a bright, adventure-seeking dream team. After dinner, Rene suggested our next cultural activity.

"Let's do a *botellón*," he said in the kitchen as Peter washed our dishes and I searched for tickets to go and visit them in the Netherlands the following month. I was making my first plan.

"What's that?" I asked, never having heard that word in my life. *Botella* means bottle, so according to my understanding of Spanish grammar, *botellón* would mean "big bottle."

"It's when you buy a fifth of alcohol, ice, and mixer and drink it out of plastic cups in a public place," he answered matter-of-factly.

"They have a word for that? In the States, that's just called getting drunk in public."

"They need a word because it's how everyone drinks here." He laughed.

We decided that our alcohol would be tequila, and our public place would be the Plaza de España. When we arrived, the blue hour was upon us, and the moon was high in the lavender sky, casting an incandescent light over the fountain. We took turns playing music on our portable speaker, exposing a little piece of our souls with each song we played. Rene sang every word to a Mumford and Sons song with his eyes closed tight and his hands clenched in a fist, and I played "Singing Joy to the World" by the Fruit Bats, letting a little tear form in my eyes when he hit my favorite note during the last line.

There was magic in the air that night. The three of us had a beautiful chemistry, like we had been three best friends our entire lives. I couldn't believe how fortunate I had been to meet these guys and feel so connected to two complete strangers all the way across the world. The tequila started to kick in, and we decided to move our sentimental *botellón* to someplace a little more interesting. We found ourselves scaling a wrought-iron fence and falling over the other side into another garden speckled with fountains. The next thing I knew, we were barefoot and knee-deep in a fountain, headbanging to Pearl Jam and splashing around in a grand celebration of life.

We ambled boisterously back through the city in the early hours of the morning, laughing and leaning on each other. Back at the hostel, I had to guide Peter up the stairs. He was a whole head taller than me and could easily have crushed my thin frame, but I held his arm forcefully and braced myself on the railing to prevent him from pulling me down. Had I out drunk this massive, burly Dutchman? I tucked him into his bunk bed and told him I'd see him in the morning. I would not, however, see him in the morning because I had already made my plans to leave Sevilla. I had bought a bus ticket for the next day to Cádiz. I wasn't trying to get comfortable anywhere. I was still searching for something that I hadn't yet found.

I woke up just a few hours later to my vibrating phone alarm, which I had put under my pillow so as not to disturb any of the other hostel guests and to avoid awkward goodbyes. My mouth was dry and tasted of tequila, and my eyes were puffy and tired. I collected my things and shoved them carelessly into my pack, and as I was just about to hoist it onto my back, I heard a muffled voice from Peter's bunk.

"Vredevoogd," he said with his head face down in his pillow. "You're leaving us."

I walked over to his bunk, quietly and carefully, and gave him a big hug. "I'll see you in Amsterdam," I whispered, and grabbing my backpack, I crept stealthily out of the room.

Cádiz

THE BUS RATTLED AS WE drove down the freeway, up and over mountains and around sharp bends, my stomach turning with each lurch forward and abrupt swerve. I was beginning to realize that I had woken up still a bit drunk on tequila and was experiencing what I had always previously referred to as the dreaded "delayed hangover." After three hours gazing as far into the horizon as I could in attempt to calm my carsickness, I clumsily got off the bus and grabbed my pack from the underneath the storage compartment.

As per usual, I had not researched the capital city of Cádiz at all. I knew it was on a small peninsula and was an old city, and I had some images of white villages and long, sandy beaches in my mind, but that was it. With my pack already on, I started feeling reluctant to take a step in any direction. Looking around me, all I saw were blonde heads, sunburnt shoulders, inner tubes, and beach chairs as crowds of tourists made their way down the sidewalk to the beach.

My hands were sweaty from the heat and my hangover, and I felt nauseous when I imagined myself bumping my way through the masses with their slimy, sunscreened arms rubbing against mine and the sun beating down on me. This was not what I wanted.

Without doubting my sudden change of heart even for a moment, I whipped around and started toward what looked like a station. Whether it was for buses or trains, I had no idea, but since now I had no specific place that I needed or wanted to be, I figured that any place would do. I walked inside and saw through the arches some train tracks and had my answer. I took out my phone, which was on its last five percent of battery, to discover that I would not be enjoying the public Wi-Fi because there wasn't any. My options were limited without Wi-Fi, so when I saw the ticket machines across the room, I walked over to press some buttons and see where I could go. There were various destinations, none of which I recognized, but for some reason, Jerez de la Frontera caught my eye. I fumbled around with the buttons and my credit card until I managed to buy a ticket, sat down with my bare legs straight out on the cool floor, and waited for my train.

It was the middle of the afternoon, and as most Spanish people were just finishing their lunch and about to relax into their siesta, I was alone in the station and then alone on the train. I didn't even know when to get off or how many stops it would be until my randomly chosen destination. After about twenty minutes of staring out the window, the train stopped for the third time, and I thought to myself, *This looks fine.* Since I had no emotional attachment to Jerez de la Frontera and had no idea when I'd arrive there, why not just get off here? Wherever here was.

I stepped off the train and looked around me. There were dusty roads and old buildings. I saw a few taxis parked near the platform and remembered a story that my friend, Katie, had told me about a terrible taxi experience she had had in Madrid where the driver locked the doors and wouldn't let her out. I shook the story out of my head and walked over to the taxis.

"*Hola. Me puede llevar al centro?*" Speaking Spanish was starting to become less stressful, although by no means easy. My heart didn't race as quickly as when I had asked the woman to watch my backpack, but I still felt like an idiot when I spoke. The taxi driver responded in Spanish that sounded like none I had ever heard before, and without waiting to see if I understood him, he began loading my pack into the trunk. He drove through small, empty streets, turning left and right in what I was too tired to realize were circles, successfully tripling our drive time and my taxi fare. I wasn't thinking about being taken advantage of as a foreigner. I wasn't thinking about money. I wasn't thinking about absolutely anything.

We pulled into a square in front of a church, and he motioned up to the meter. I paid and got out. I slowly looked around. This was the center?

There were nine pigeons picking at the ground, one elderly man in a flat cap and tweed sitting on a bench observing the church, and one woman pulling chairs out of a bar for the two tables she had brought outside to the sidewalk. This place was different than anywhere I had ever been. It was ancient and quiet. It reminded me of some of the small villages in Mexico I had visited over the years of family holidays, especially during the siesta hour when time seemed to stop. I remembered how lonely I would sometimes feel during the siesta in Mexico as everyone else, including most of my family, took their afternoon nap, which is an art that I was never able to master. I had felt like I was the only person left in the world after some sudden natural disaster that had wiped out the rest of the population. It was that still. It was the contrast of that stillness with the music and commotion of all other hours of the day that disconcerted me as a little girl.

I sat down on the other bench to the right of the man and looked up at the church, just as he was. What was he seeing in that building? I was not raised Catholic so its spiritual glory didn't stir anything deep within me, and I was curious about the feelings that were being awakened for the old man because they seemed to inspire him to spend his afternoons staring up at that cross against the bright blue Andalusian sky.

I stood up and hauled my pack over to the only other person in my radius and sat down at one of the plastic tables. I ordered a glass of gazpacho, a healthy and reenergizing tomato and garlic drink, which seemed appropriate after my unhealthy night and arduous afternoon. To my surprise, the woman came back out of the bar and placed a small plate of olives, bread, and cheese in front of me. I had discovered the authentic tapas: the small plates of food that are just gifted to you with every drink you order. After savoring every bite and enjoying every sip, I awkwardly and unhurriedly thudded my way down the street, hopeful that I'd find a place to sleep. More than hopeful, I was expectant, as the possibility of not finding a place to sleep was not something I considered to be a real danger—however real it may have been.

I plodded down the street, eyeing the buildings that lined the sidewalk, completely aware that a Starbucks with Wi-Fi was not going to appear in front of me, and yet still hoping that it would. The streets were desolate. I walked past an elderly woman sitting next to her ground floor window with her two small dogs next to her, pressing their noses against the glass as she knit. A thin, ponytailed man with a guitar on his back and a cigarette hanging from his lips swaggered by, singing flamenco while smoke snaked out of his mouth. I kept plodding down the cobblestone street. The buildings were old, ancient even, and unkempt. Broken windowpanes dotted the graffitied exteriors of abandoned apartments, and alley cats darted in and out of the busted doors. This place was melancholy, but beautiful. As I continued, I began to notice fewer graffiti, fewer broken windows, then a restaurant, then a few people, and then a hostel.

I opened the door and the man at the desk looked up at me from the book he was reading. I began my conversation with him in Spanish, and he quickly made an executive decision to switch over to English, although whether his English was in fact better than my Spanish was debatable. There was a private room available and I settled right in. It would be my first time in weeks sleeping alone in a room to myself. After resting, I grabbed my camera and hit the streets, reminding myself to pay attention to landmarks or buildings with interesting graffiti in order to find my way back. I wandered through the maze of empty alleyways, feeling alone without feeling lonely. The sun softly touched the horizon, and just as the blue hour fell upon Puerto de Santa María, I turned a corner and everything changed. There were tables full of people lining the streets, laughter and exuberant conversations echoing all around, and musicians singing and strumming their guitars. How had one right turn changed my reality so completely?

I walked slowly down the avenue of bars and pubs, watching the faces of the people around me. There were endless groups of young adults in bohemian-chic outfits with huge smiles on their faces, and their tables were full of beers and food. At this moment, I began to feel like an outsider. I wanted a beer, but I couldn't imagine myself sitting down to occupy a table alone while being surrounded by so much joy and comradery in which I couldn't participate. I had never been one to avoid eating alone in restaurants or drinking alone in bars in fear of what people might think—it was actually second nature to me—and I was perturbed that I felt self-conscious about sitting down alone. I saw an empty table amidst more of those happy, laughing people that so much reminded me of my friends back in Bellingham, and I decided to quiet my insecurity in one fell swoop. I sat down and ordered a beer.

After another beer, I took a walk along the port. There was a carnival happening on the promenade, and I stopped to admire the tables full of artisan goods. I bought myself a turquoise necklace because it just seemed right in the moment, and then I leisurely followed the graffiti back to the hostel.

The next morning, I woke up with a peculiar feeling. I could do whatever I wanted, and I didn't have to tell anyone about it. I could laze about my room, writing and fiddling around on Photoshop between naps. I could go exploring nearby towns and villages in the province of Cádiz. I could go to the bar in the plaza and drink ten beers and wait for something exciting to happen because, after all, that's what I was doing—waiting for something to happen.

In the end, I decided to find the beach. I knew it was near because I had seen it during the train ride, but I didn't know in which direction I'd have to walk in order to find it. I started in one direction, and after asking a woman for the "*playa*," I turned completely around and followed where her finger had been pointing, without veering from that trajectory for forty minutes, until I had a long, sandy beach sprawling in front of me. I had reached paradise.

I stopped at a fruit stand before making the trek down the hill and then across the sand toward the water. I stood there in the tiny shop, wedged in-between the little old women with cloth carts on wheels who were nudging and elbowing each other, vying for the attention of the greengrocer. When my turn was up, I panicked. I knew I wanted two apples, a banana, some tomatoes, and an avocado, but I had no idea how to make that happen. The greengrocer asked me how many kilos I wanted, and I realized that I was lost as to how many kilos of apples were two apples. After struggling for a few minutes, and thanks to the help of one of the elbowing women, who was clearly only helping me so that her turn would come more quickly, I left the fruit stand with an assortment of produce, still unsure of how many kilos I had in the bag.

I spent the day under the sun, admiring the Atlantic Ocean from the opposite side that I had been just days before with Miette. As I contemplated this change of perspective, I imagined myself turn into a little point on a map, and as the map grew bigger and zoomed father out, my little point disappeared into nothing. I was so far away from my world, the bubble in which I grew up in the Pacific Northwest, and nobody from that world knew where I was. None of my friends or family members knew that I was sitting alone on a beach in Puerto de Santa María in the South of Spain, and this fact made me feel alive. I felt free of responsibilities and explanations. Free of judgment and worry. Free of consequence. Free.

I went back to the beach the following day, and the day after, and the day after that. I had my ritual of sipping a coffee just outside my hostel and then stopping at the same fruit stand, each day ordering my bag of snacks more efficiently and effectively until I could indicate what I wanted by the quarter kilo. Then I made the journey to the same spot on the beach, where I would read, swim, dry off, read, and then swim some more until the sun went down. It was a healing week that recharged my spirit. During that week, I didn't worry about where I was going or what I was supposed to do when the trip was over. I only used my phone to listen to music, uninspired to speak to anyone, although the messages I received were sparse anyways.

When my time in Puerto was up, I could feel it. A voice whispered in my ear, "It's time to move on," and I knew I needed to go. I jumped on my laptop and remembered a city called Granada that a girl whom I had worked with in an upscale lounge years before had spoken about. She had recently returned from a year abroad and was trying to reintegrate herself back into her previous life, although the reverse culture shock had proven challenging. She told me that Granada was her favorite hidden corner in the world. I remembered the longing in her eyes as she said it, and I bought the ticket to Granada for the following morning.

Granada

I FELT SERENE AFTER MY WEEK in Puerto de Santa María. The colors of the landscape out the bus window were toasted greens and golden browns, and the sky was a radiant blue. I spent the hours reading *Magical Thinking* by Augusten Burroughs and listening to Portishead without resisting the tears that formed in my eyes over the divine combination of music and prose. I devoured the pages, shocked by how emotionally invested I was in the memoir and how deeply I was able to empathize with the protagonist. Near the end of the book, there was a passage about unconditional love, which hit something so deep inside my rib cage that for a moment I couldn't breathe.

I had my feet up on the empty seat next to me and was leaning my head against the window, cushioned by my Pismo. I wore my giant sunglasses to hide the cascade of tears rolling down my cheeks. I wasn't sure if I was crying with joy that the author had managed to find love again, in appreciation of how beautiful it was to love, or if this passage had somehow drawn my attention to how utterly alone I was on that bus in the south of Spain. I wondered if anyone, besides Miette, had ever truly known me enough to love me unconditionally.

I carefully started pulling the page out of the binding, and then I made a crease where the passage ended and tore it out. I didn't care that I was defaming a piece of literature. I needed to keep this passage with me. I needed to remember that feeling of empathy, joy, and loneliness all mashed together in a way that pinched my soul and made my organs quiver. I reread it, then carefully rolled it up, and placed it inside my little silver pouch from New Orleans, which contained my moonstone and a coin I had found on the ground in Sevilla. This would be my pouch of amulets.

The bus pulled into the bus station in Granada at one in the afternoon. It was sweltering hot. I followed the crowds out of the station and to a bus and taxi stop in front, unsure of where I was supposed to go exactly. I had rented a bed in a hostel, which was supposedly near the cathedral, which I imagined would be in the city center, but I hadn't looked at any maps to confirm this. I got on a bus which said *Estacion de Autobuses/ Centro* and figured that it was as good as any.

The bus was packed and stuffy. We drove into the city, and I waited to see a cathedral so I would know when to get off. I saw some old buildings and some ornate churches, but were they cathedrals? I wasn't sure. I eventually asked a young woman who was in the seat behind me. In a Spanish which sounded a bit different from the Spanish I had heard in Puerto—although my ears weren't finely tuned enough to know exactly how it was different—she told me that the stop for the cathedral was the one behind us and that I should get off at the next one.

I pulled out my instructions for arriving to Hostel Oasis. I followed Gran Vía, the main avenue, to a narrow street, where a row of dark-skinned men sold tea and brightly-colored spices in bulk from baskets underneath a colossal structure, which I assumed to be the cathedral. I was still in flip-flops, and as I walked down the hill, I could feel my feet sliding around on the smooth stones of the sidewalk, nearly slipping out from beneath me and throwing me to the ground on various occasions.

I arrived at a beautiful square, and thanks to the fountain and the shade of the trees, it was the perfect place to cool down and reevaluate my route. I studied the map and realized that I had turned down off of Gran Vía when I should have turned up. Without an ounce of hurry, I slipped my arms into the sweaty straps of my pack, which was on the bench next to me, and pulled myself up. I trudged back up the street I had just walked down, crossed Gran Vía, and found the street sign I was looking for: Calderería.

Calderería was a narrow, pedestrian street with broad stone steps that curved back and forth up a steep hill. On each side were small shops selling Arabic pastries and Moroccan imports, alternating with Arabic tea houses adorned with richly-colored sofas next to knee high tables, each one with a silver shisha in the middle. The edges of the street were dotted with men in robes and pointy leather slippers, sitting on sparkling cushions and shouting to one another in Arabic. Was this still Spain? If I had opened my eyes after having been transported to this place, I would have thought I was in North Africa or Turkey. In reality, North Africa was just a few hours away.

I studied the intricate stained-glass lamps hanging in the shops and vibrant throws decorating the streets as I walked up the steps, careful not to bump into anyone or anything with my monstrous backpack. After arriving at the hostel and checking in, I found my bunk upstairs in an empty room with four beds. The hostel was a labyrinth of stairs, rooms, and patios. I had been lucky to be assigned this room because all of the other rooms I had passed were packed with travelers, squeezed in their bunks like sardines. I peered out the window to see an outdoor patio on the ground floor. There were tables around which sat interesting-looking people who were laughing, drinking, and playing guitar. I tucked away my things and went to check it out.

I walked into the patio to find a tall, red-haired, and rosy-nosed Irishman behind the bar muddling mint for an order of mojitos and a crowd of kids chatting, smoking, and enjoying the bohemian lifestyle that Granada seemed to inspire. I took a seat where I usually felt most comfortable—right at the bar.

"Would you like a mojito?" asked the Irish kid. I've always loved Irish accents, people who spoke with them always sounded like they were having fun, even when they were telling you where to go or where to put something.

"I think I'll take a beer actually. Thanks," I said, fiddling with my lighter.

"Not big on the cocktails then," he replied, pulling out a cold bottle from the cooler. "You want to open it?" he asked, nodding at my lighter, challenging me to open my beer with it, which I did effortlessly.

"Atta girl. I'm Leo. Who are you?"

"I'm Kate."

A girl sitting a little farther down the bar overheard us and chimed in, "Leo and Kate. Like Titanic! That is so perfect!"

The sun set over the patio, and the string of lights around the stone wall softly illuminated the smiling faces they surrounded. Exhausted after a long day of traveling, I soon went up to my room and fell asleep, not to wake up until afternoon the following day.

When I finally rolled myself out of bed, it was nearly two o'clock. I felt groggy and out of sorts after having slept for over twelve hours so I pulled my hair back in a messy ponytail and threw on the first wrinkled tank and shorts I could find in my backpack. As I entered Calderería for the second time, I felt conflicted. It was like I was meant to be there but also like I still didn't quite fit in. It was still so obvious that I had just arrived.

I walked into the first tapas bar I came across, and when I ordered my coffee, the waiter looked puzzled. In Granada, beer is the expected drink order any time after noon because that's when the free tapas start, but what was I supposed to do if I woke up late? First coffee, then beer.

After finishing my coffee and now feeling a bit more awake, I walked back down to the cathedral because I hadn't spent much time appreciating its grandeur. I had never seen a cathedral so big. I gazed at the beautiful gothic architecture as I circled around the massive building, feeling miniscule below it. Next, I took a walk up to Plaza Nueva and drank fresh horchata next to the fountain, close enough for the mist to cool my skin. There was a soft electricity in the streets of Granada that hummed with creativity.

Back at the hostel hours later, I decided to try one of Leo's famous mojitos. The same bohemian atmosphere from the night before filled the patio. "You want to work tonight?" Leo asked after chatting through the first half of my drink.

"What? Like bartending?"

"No, doing a pub crawl." I had never been on a pub crawl, much less been a guide for one, not to mention that I had only just arrived at Granada and hadn't even been to a bar yet.

I winced, because apart from my lack of qualifications for the job, I knew that pub crawls were not my scene. Leo continued, "It's basically just glorified babysitting. I normally go with Jack, but he's really hung-over today and is being a cunt about it." His casual use of the word "cunt" jolted me. *It must be an Irish thing,* I thought.

"What would I have to do?"

"Just help me herd the kids and make sure none of them vomit anywhere they shouldn't until three a.m. when they can vomit anywhere they please. It's easy. Just come for fuck's sake."

I thought about his offer and decided that it was one of those "why not?" situations and accepted. I needed to be in the bar at ten, ready to babysit, so I had an hour and a half to kill.

I sucked down the last sugary drops of my mojito and decided to go to the viewpoint, San Miguel Alto, to watch the sunset, which I had heard some people talking about earlier. I set out with my camera up the narrow, winding streets of the Albayzín neighborhood. It was a maze of white buildings and uneven cobblestone streets. Beautiful magenta flowers spilled over the stark white sides of the houses, and flowerpots hung from the walls and balconies. I kept climbing up and up, unsure of exactly where I was going or how to get there until I was eventually in a clearing above the city. I turned around and saw Granada before me. I continued up a long series of steps until, panting and dripping with sweat, I reached San Miguel Alto.

It was an old building that looked like a church with

a low stone wall in front of it, on which people were sitting, contemplating the sunset. A group of friends sat cross-legged on a Moroccan blanket and were playing flamenco guitar and singing softly, their music creating a perfect soundtrack for the moment. I looked out over the city and played *Where's Waldo?* with the cathedral. I was above it all, like a bird in a nest. I felt like a part of something, like these people around me were my friends, like we were all there together. The sky was the warmest, creamiest color of gold I had ever seen. I lifted up my camera and took my first picture in Granada, which turned out to be the most beautiful image I had made to date.

There was no doubt in my mind that this place was enchanted by a wise and ancient magic. I could feel the passion of the *gitanos*—an ethnic group linked to the nomadic Roma people—who had stomped and howled their pain and heartbreak through flamenco music for years in the caves of the Sacromonte. I felt the inspiration of all of the artists and writers who had woven stories and made beautiful creations here. I was taken over by the wanderlust of all the bohemians who had come by chance and never left. I closed my eyes and breathed in the smell of toasted earth and incense, and I opened them just in time to see the sun disappear behind the mountains. This place was different than anywhere I had ever been. This was where I was supposed to be. This was where I was going to stay.

Epilogue

I AM SITTING IN THE LEATHER chair next to the Christmas tree at my parents' house in Bellingham. I am looking out at the frost-covered grass and bare, spindly cottonwood trees. I have the hood of my Pismo sweatshirt bunched up around my neck. I lift up my steaming coffee to take a sip and watch a red-tailed hawk plunge headfirst toward the ground. It is the morning of the last day of 2018, and it's my first time home during the winter in five years.

My phone vibrates on the wooden armrest. It's my Spanish friend, Alex, wishing me "Happy New Year" since it's already early evening in Granada. I send him an audio message in my now fluent Spanish, with a noticeable Andalusian accent, saying that I'm excited to see him when I get home next week. I sigh and continue observing the birds.

My phone vibrates again, but this time it's Miette sending me a picture of her youngest son in his reindeer jammies with a big, toothless grin on his squishy little face. She sends another with the whole family: Miette, Sol, two-year-old Oskar, and six-month-old Roland in the lovely house they own in Moses Lake, Washington. Fixing their relationship was not an easy undertaking for either of them. In fact, it took two years of living in New Jersey and focusing on each other before they felt solid enough to move back to Washington and start their family. Just as the tea-reader in New Orleans had said, they put in the work, and they found happiness together.

I've gotten used to yelling over the background of shrieking children and cartoons during our bi-weekly phone calls. She is such a dedicated mother, but it's still strange for me to think about how different the paths are that we each chose for our lives. That moment in Boston when I got out of the car was the point where the tree branch split in two directions, but each new branch still comes from the same roots. I have only seen her in the flesh four times since she dropped me off at the airport five years ago, but somehow she is closer to me than ever before, and our roots will always be here in the countryside where we grew up together, running from goblins in the evergreen forest.

The sun is out, and it is beginning to melt the ice on the lawn. I think about how lucky we are to have had a sunny Christmas and now a sunny New Year's Eve in a place that is known for nine months of rain per year. I plan to take the dog out for a hike on the logging trails where Miette and I always used to take walks and work out our problems. After that, I'll do some post-production that I've been putting off for a photography shoot I did recently. Above the couch, where my parents' dog is stretched out, is a large wooden print of that first photo I took in Granada at San Miguel Alto. Every time I see it, I relive the magic of that evening. Looking at the dog makes me miss my sweet Catalan Shepherd, Laila, who is back in Granada waiting for my return. I adopted her two years ago when she was just a month old, and she may not know this, but she's changed the entire course of my life. She probably knows it. That's probably why she found me.

I feel good here. Normally when I come home to Washington to visit in August, I bring with me a full year of distance from my friends and family. I struggle to reintegrate myself in the routine and balance my social commitments with necessary family time and me time. But I was just here four months ago. I don't feel the pressure to see all of the people who I won't see for another year or eat all of the food whose flavors I won't enjoy for another year. I'm just here, quietly watching the birds flit from tree branch to tree branch, wrapping myself up in a blanket of nostalgia, and letting myself get cozy.

Exactly five and a half years ago, I said goodbye to my parents in this very room and drove away. Everything has changed since then. For one, my relationship with them is stronger and more authentic than it's ever been. Because I live so far away, I understand that if I don't take care of our connection, it will fade and eventually be reduced to birthday and holiday check-ins.

I also understand that this is true with friendships, and I now have friends that I would upgrade to the family category, even though they live thousands of miles away. I wouldn't say I have things figured out, and I don't think I ever will, but that's the thing about living: it's not a struggle until one day you figure it all out and then it's done—you've won at life. No. You never stop having to figure things out, but once you accept that, it can stop feeling like a struggle or a problem that has to be solved. Once you stop trying to solve life, you can start living in the moment. For me, it's become about going with the flow but in a more conscious way, exploring opportunities but empowering myself to only pursue those that resonate with me, forgiving myself for making mistakes, and making sure those mistakes have been worthwhile by learning from each and every one.

Five years ago, I would never have imagined that right now I'd be living in Southern Spain working as a photographer and ESL teacher, completely bilingual and having traveled all over Europe, which makes me wonder about those five-year plans people talk about. My five-year plan right now is to be somewhere, simultaneously learning and feeling fulfilled, and not knowing where I'll be five years from then.

Thank you for reading my story. I kindly invite you to share your comments and reactions with your favorite retailer—or with me directly, if you feel inspired.

About the Author

Kate Vredevoogd was born in Bellingham, Washington, where she grew up in the countryside with her loving parents and her many animal friends. She is deeply afflicted by wanderlust, which is why she spent six years in Granada working as a freelance photographer and traveling around Europe. She currently lives in Málaga, Spain. *From the Same Quiver* is her first publication.

katevredevoogd.com
instagram.com/kateinspain/

˒SIA information can be obtained
˒w.ICGtesting.com
˙in the USA
˒010080421